don't miss the
BOAT

don't miss the
BOAT

Facts to Keep Your Faith Afloat

Paul Taylor

First printing: June 2013

Master Books®, P.O. Box 726, Green Forest, AR 72638

Master Books® is a division of the New Leaf Publishing Group, Inc.

ISBN: 978-0-89051-721-5

Library of Congress Number: 2013941179

Cover by Diana Bogardus

Image credits: Answers in Genesis:123 (top), 124; Biblicalgeology.net: 149; Creation.com: 144; Shutterstock: 46, 142; Vectorworldmap.com: 85; Wikimedia Commons: 45 (right), 51, 78, 79, 84, 90, 101, 123 (bottom), 150, 151 (both), 156, 157 (top and bottom); Wikipedia: 143; Worldwideflood.com: 119, 120

Unless otherwise noted, Scripture quotations are from the New King James Version of the Bible.

Please consider requesting that a copy of this volume be purchased by your local library system.

Printed in the United States of America

Please visit our website for other great titles:
www.masterbooks.net

For information regarding author interviews,
please contact the publicity department at (870) 438-5288

Master
Books®
A Division of New Leaf Publishing Group
www.masterbooks.net

Contents

Introduction

Since the creation of the universe, one of the most significant events in history was the Flood. Yet this world-changing event is today ridiculed and scorned — as are those who accept its historicity. Most people would, today, prefer to suggest that the account of the Flood in Genesis 6–9 is at best a clever allegory, and most probably ranks alongside stories like *Cinderella* and *Sleeping Beauty*.

Regrettably, so-called conservative evangelical churches have led the way, in recent years, in compiling a theology of doubt. Driven by fear of ridicule or lack of academic respectability, conservative evangelicals have become ever more imaginative in their efforts to harmonize the Scriptures with old-age geology and evolutionary biology. While they do this, the atheists are ever more vociferous in pointing out (rightly, in my view) that it is not possible to believe both the Bible and evolutionary theory. However, so many of these conservative evangelicals have invested so much theological capital in accepting evolutionary and old-earth ideas as truthful that the only position to give must be their adherence to biblical truth. Of course, as conservative evangelicals they cannot admit to disbelief in the Bible, so they have to resort to fuzzy phrases, such as "we need to understand who the book was written for," or "this book was written for an age that was scientifically illiterate," and "God had to explain these truths in language that the people would understand." One must suppose that the language that people would understand must be lies.

This author believes the Flood to have been a real, historical event. The evidence left behind by this event is enormous, and can be seen in the huge quantities of sedimentary rock all over the world. But secular scientists prefer to interpret their observations in the light of their presupposition that the earth is billions of years old and that God had little, if anything, to do with the creation of the rocks.

Doubts Predicted by Peter

Doubts about the Flood were famously prophesied by the Apostle Peter in his second epistle.

> Know this first: that scoffers will come in the last days, walking according to their own lusts, and saying, "Where is the promise of His coming? For since the fathers fell asleep, all things continue as they were from the beginning of creation." For this they willfully forget: that by the word of God the heavens were of old, and the earth standing out of water and in the water, by which the world that then existed perished, being flooded with water (2 Peter 3:3–6).

The scoffers "willfully forget" two matters — the historicity of the creation week and the historicity of the Flood. In doing so, they cannot cope with the wealth of evidence available for both these events; because the evidence does not fit into their paradigm, they ignore it.

Books about the Flood

There have been a number of good books about the Flood in the past. Indeed, the modern creationist movement was kick-started by just such a book with the 1961 publication of *The Genesis Flood*, by John Whitcomb and Henry Morris. In recent years, Dr. Andrew Snelling has updated this classic, under a new title — *Earth's Catastrophic Past*. Many of the learned scientific articles in the peer-reviewed creationist journals concentrate on issues to do with the Flood.

There are also very good chapters about aspects to do with the Flood in many of the general creationist books that can be found in local Christian bookstores.

What we seem to lack is a book that is both easy-to-read and comprehensive in its treatment of the subject. This book aims to fill that gap.

A Fascinating Subject

I have always found the Flood to be a fascinating subject, and I love to talk about it in my seminars. The account of the Flood really has everything. It has drama, relationship issues, theology, science, and the gospel. It is my desire to capture these threads. However, I have indeed seen them as threads. The person wanting to learn some of the theology of the Flood does not necessarily want to get bogged down with the science.

In this book, I have endeavored to clearly label the sort of content that you will find in each chapter. The first section of the book contains chapters that are expositions. Science is kept to a minimum. Great concentration is placed on the *typology* found in the account.

The second section contains historical articles. It focuses on ancient history, in the immediate post-Flood period as well as the history of how old-earth compromises came to be accepted.

After this, we have a section on science. I kept this section separate because the science is, at the same time, both popular and unpopular. For some, the scientific information is what makes the subject interesting. For others, being blinded with technicalities is undesirable, so it should be possible for such people to skip or skim through this section. It should also be pointed out that I have simplified the science as much as is possible. Those who want more detailed science should get Dr. Snelling's book.

I wanted to be able to relate something of the emotional power of God's judgment coming on a wicked pre-Flood world. After much consideration, I decided that the most effective way of achieving this would be to have a fictional section, so the fourth section contains four monologues by pre-Flood characters.

As with most parts of God's Word, this account is really about the gospel of Jesus Christ. When I make such a statement, there will be some who will worry that I am about to treat the account allegorically. I am not. I treat it *typologically*. A *type* is not a metaphor. It is something that is real, but that also has spiritual significance. For example, it is well known that the Passover is a type of the death of Jesus. To say that does not imply that the Passover never happened. Of course it happened. But God designed it to also teach about the necessity of the sacrificial Lamb of God.

So the last paragraph is a long-winded justification for the fact that I have included an article entitled "The Gospel According to Noah" so that the reader can understand how the typology of the Flood relates to the gospel.

Finally, I want people to be able to study the whole subject of the Flood. So the last section is a study guide that can be used for individual study or for small groups. It could be that small groups want to concentrate on a program led by the expositions, rather than chapter by chapter, so it should be possible to mix and match the questions in whatever order you require.

And Finally . . .

I have really enjoyed putting this book together. I hope that you will enjoy reading it and learning from it, and maybe graduating to study some of the more technical works about the Flood. In the meantime, watch out for the DVD series that will accompany the book.

May God bless you as you study His Word.

Paul Taylor, BSc MEd
Director of Ministry Development
Creation Today

Chapter 1

The World before the Flood

Genesis 6:1–2

Jesus reminded us that before the Flood most people were not expecting it.

> But as the days of Noah were, so also will the coming of the Son of Man be. For as in the days before the flood, they were eating and drinking, marrying and giving in marriage, until the day that Noah entered the ark, and did not know until the flood came and took them all away, so also will the coming of the Son of Man be (Matthew 24:37–39).

We can, of course, feel quite smug about the level of non-expectation and antediluvian apathy. Yet Jesus was using the account of the Flood as a true-life analogy of what His own Second Coming would be like. He was suggesting to His hearers that they "watch" (Matthew 24:42) and "be ready" (Matthew 24:44), so that, even though they would not know the exact timetable, they would be ready for the most important event in history. Yet we know that the majority of people in the world will be completely oblivious to the coming of Jesus, until it happens. In the same way, the world before the Flood was warned that it was going to happen, and was advised to be ready, but they paid no heed. Learning about the state of the world immediately before the Flood is, therefore, a good training ground for getting ready for Jesus' Second Coming. His Second Coming will be a one-of-a-kind event, and it hasn't happened yet. But the Flood has already happened and, because Jesus Himself made the comparison, we would do well to study what happened the first time God decided to end the world.

Chapter 6 Follows Chapter 4

Genesis chapter 5 was a brief interlude for Moses to record the promised line of descent, which we now know eventually ended up with the Messiah. So the introductory phrase of the sixth chapter — "Now it came to pass . . ." — is basically a continuation of the thoughts in the last verse of chapter 4.

> And as for Seth, to him also a son was born; and he named him Enosh. Then men began to call on the name of the LORD (Genesis 4:26).

The latter half of Genesis 4 records how the descendants of Cain had sunk to new lows of depravity. Take the case of Lamech, who gleefully compared himself to his great-great-great-grandfather, the world's first murderer.

> Then Lamech said to his wives: "Adah and Zillah, hear my voice; wives of Lamech, listen to my speech! For I have killed a man for wounding me, even a young man for hurting me. If Cain shall be avenged sevenfold, then Lamech seventy-sevenfold" (Genesis 4:23–24).

Even wicked Cain only married one wife. Lamech's sexual needs ran to two. With an exponentially expanding early population, there was no numerical requirement for Lamech to have two wives. We can only assume, therefore, that his sin of bigamy was itself the result of a deeply sinful heart. This sinful nature is exposed by his self-comparison with Cain. Cain was a murderer, because of his jealousy. He knew that his crime was wrong. Lamech positively boasted about how he killed a man, just for wounding him. This was a "punishment" above and beyond what was appropriate. Note also that Lamech decided that his act of murder was really an act of justice. But God did not, and has not, sanctioned the individual to carry out the execution of murderers on their own behalf, and still less the execution of someone who has merely "wounded" one. As a bunny trail, the above comment should not be seen as an argument against the death penalty. We will return to the death penalty in our studies on Genesis, but for now it can be stated that I believe Scripture teaches that execution for murder is the correct and appropriate response. However, that execution should be carried out by society, not by the individual.

God promised that Cain would be avenged "sevenfold" if he were harmed (Genesis 4:15). Lamech, on the other hand, had decided that he could do better than God. He decided that he could set his own target (seventy-sevenfold) and that he could carry out the execution of that target himself, whereas, in Cain's place, the punishment, if required, would have been administered by God.

In summary, Lamech decided that he could disobey God's command in the following ways: he could set his own number of wives in defiance of God's plans; he could carry out his own executions rather than leaving them to a society under God; and he could make his own threats about how he would offensively defend himself (if "offensively defend" can be considered to be a proper terminology).

This evil legacy, which had developed among the descendants of Cain, can be contrasted with an alternative legacy that grew among the descendants of Seth.

> Then *men* began to call on the name of the Lord (Genesis 4:26).

The context of this verse suggests that it was the descendants of Seth who were calling on the name of the Lord. The Hebrew does not use the word "men," which is why it is in italics. Therefore, the phrase is really referring to the first half of the verse — that is, the descendants of Seth and Enosh, Seth's son. In later generations, it would not be inevitable that those in the promised lineage would necessarily be righteous worshipers of God. Indeed, the earth's population at the time of the Flood must have included many unrighteous sons of Seth. We know, after all, that Noah had brothers and sisters (Genesis 5:30). Even so, in these early years, it is likely that the ones calling on the name of the Lord would be those associated with Seth and the promised lineage. It is likely that the phrase refers to a gathering for worshiping the Lord. There is even a possibility that the phrase really implies that men "were calling themselves by the name of the Lord," as we might refer to ourselves as Christians — followers of Christ.

Sons of God and Daughters of Men

This brings us to the sons of God and the daughters of men — two concepts that have caused endless amounts of frustration for centuries. The key to understanding these concepts, however, would appear to be to remember, as I stated before, that the narrative of Genesis 6 follows the narrative of Genesis 4 — Genesis 5 being an interlude when the genealogy of the promised lineage is recorded. In that case, it would seem likely to me that the term "sons of God" is referring to that group of people who were collectively worshiping the Lord — that is, the descendants of Seth. If that is so, then the "daughters of men" refers to descendants of Cain. Remember that Cain and Seth were not the only children of Adam and Eve. There were plenty of "other sons and daughters" (Genesis 5:4) from whom marriages could be contracted. Those who claimed to be worshipers of the Lord, however, should not have been intermarrying with those who were usurping God's role — which is what Cainite people like Lamech were doing. Therefore, the fact that the marriages between the sons of God and the daughters of men appeared to be problematic, puts one in mind of the New Testament injunction:

> Do not be unequally yoked together with unbelievers. For what fellowship has righteousness with lawlessness? And what communion has light with darkness? (2 Cor. 6:14; see Deut. 7:3, Gen. 24:3–4).

This interpretation is not the most common among modern creationists. Many modern creationists see evidence of angelic, or rather demonic, activity at play. It is important to acknowledge two facts about the angelic interpretation. First is that this is not the most important point of doctrine or biblical interpretation, and I would be unlikely to separate myself from someone who believed that the sons of God were fallen angels. Second, we should acknowledge that there is a certain amount of circumstantial biblical support for the demonic hypothesis — the phrase "sons of God" is used elsewhere in Scripture to describe angels; for example, Job 38:7. It would appear, however, that the concept of the Genesis 6 "sons of God" being fallen angels owes its origins not to Genesis 6, which I argue does not support such a view, but to the apocryphal books of Jubilees and Enoch.

In the Book of Jubilees, we read:

> And it came to pass when the children of men began to multiply on the face of the earth and daughters were born unto them, that the angels of God saw them on a certain year of this jubilee, that they were beautiful to look upon; and they took themselves wives of all whom they chose, and they bare unto them sons and they were giants. And lawlessness increased on the earth and all

flesh corrupted its way, alike men and cattle and beasts and birds and everything that walks on the earth — all of them corrupted their ways and their orders, and they began to devour each other, and lawlessness increased on the earth and every imagination of the thoughts of all men (was) thus evil continually.[1]

In this passage, we read the idea that the offspring of this unnatural union between demons and humans were the giants. However, I will show in a moment that the giants were something different.

The book of Enoch says:

And they took wives for themselves and everyone chose for himself one each. And they began to go into them and were promiscuous with them. And they taught them charms and spells, and they showed them the cutting of roots and trees. And they became pregnant and bore large giants. And their height was three thousand cubits.[2]

Facts noted in the Bible are factual. These lines from the book of Enoch cannot be factual. For example, how could there be giants "three thousand cubits" tall? We are surprised by the Bible's description of Goliath as being "six cubits and a span" (1 Samuel 17:4, about 9 feet, 9 inches, or about three meters), but it is not so large as to be unrealistic. Three thousand cubits is simply way over the top. So we should take the non-biblical interpretations that we receive from these apocryphal books with more than a little pinch of salt.

To return to my interpretation of "sons of God" as being the descendants of Seth, let's see what other major commentators had to say.

John Calvin (1509–1564) said:

It was, therefore, base ingratitude in the posterity of Seth, to mingle themselves with the children of Cain, and with other profane races; because they voluntarily deprived themselves of the inestimable grace of God. For it was an intolerable profanation, to pervert, and to confound, the order appointed by God. It seems at first sight frivolous, that the sons of God should be so severely condemned, for having chosen for themselves beautiful wives from

1. Jubilees 5:1, Wellesley Internet Archive, http://www.archive.org/details/bookofjubileesor-00char, pdf edition, p. 43, accessed 1/10/2012.
2. 1 Enoch 7:1–2, Wellesley Internet Archive, http://www.archive.org/details/AllTheBooksOfEnochenoch1Enoch2Enoch3, pdf edition, p. 5, accessed 1/10/2012.

the daughters of men. But we must know first, that it is not a light crime to violate a distinction established by the Lord; secondly, that for the worshippers of God to be separated from profane nations, was a sacred appointment which ought reverently to have been observed, in order that a Church of God might exist upon earth; thirdly, that the disease was desperate, seeing that men rejected the remedy divinely prescribed for them.[3]

Calvin went on to comment on the idea that the "sons of God" were angels.

That ancient figment, concerning the intercourse of angels with women, is abundantly refuted by its own absurdity; and it is surprising that learned men should formerly have been fascinated by ravings so gross and prodigious. The opinion also of the Chaldean paraphrase is frigid; namely, that promiscuous marriages between the sons of nobles, and the daughters of plebeians, is condemned. Moses, then, does not distinguish the sons of God from the daughters of men, because they were of dissimilar nature, or of different origin; but because they were the sons of God by adoption, whom he had set apart for himself; while the rest remained in their original condition.[4]

John Gill (1697–1771) had this to say:

Those "sons of God" were not angels either good or bad, as many have thought, since they are incorporeal beings, and cannot be affected with fleshly lusts, or marry and be given in marriage, or generate and be generated; nor the sons of judges, magistrates, and great personages, nor they themselves, as the Targums of Onkelos and Jonathan, and so Jarchi and Aben Ezra; but this could be no crime in them, to look upon and take in marriage such persons, though they were the daughters of the meaner sort; and supposing they acted a criminal part in looking at them, and lusting after them, and committing fornication with them, and even in marrying irreligious persons; yet this could only be a partial, not an universal corruption, as is after affirmed, though such examples must

---

3. John Calvin, *Commentary on Genesis*, comment on Genesis 6, Christian Classics Ethereal Library, http://www.ccel.org/ccel/calvin/calcom01.xii.i.html, accessed 1/10/2012.
4. Ibid.

indeed have great influence upon the populace; but rather this is to be understood of the posterity of Seth, who from the times of Enos, when they began to be called by the name of the Lord, had the title of the sons of God, in distinction from the children of men; these claimed the privilege of divine adoption, and professed to be born of God, and partakers of his grace, and pretended to worship him according to his will, so far as revealed to them, and to fear and serve and glorify him.[5]

Matthew Henry (1662–1714) said:

Mixed marriages (v. 2): *The sons of God* (that is, the professors of religion, who were called by the name of the Lord, and called upon that name), *married the daughters of men,* that is, those that were profane, and strangers to God and godliness. The posterity of Seth did not keep by themselves, as they ought to have done, both for the preservation of their own purity and in detestation of the apostasy. They intermingled themselves with the excommunicated race of Cain: *They took them wives of all that they chose.* But what was amiss in these marriages? (1.) They chose only by the eye: *They saw that they were fair,* which was all they looked at. (2.) They followed the choice which their own corrupt affections made: they took *all that they chose,* without advice and consideration. But, (3.) That which proved of such bad consequence to them was that they *married strange wives, were unequally yoked with unbelievers.*[6]

John Bunyan (1628–1688) had the same teaching.

By this then, I find, that the doctrine of Noah, was, To declare against a sinful communion, or to command the church, in the name of God, that she still maintain a separation from the cursed children of Cain: As he said to the prophet Jeremiah, If thou separate the precious from the vile, "thou shalt be as my mouth" (15:19). Noah therefore had a hard task, when he preached this doctrine among them: for this above all is hard to be borne, for by this he condemned the world. The first great quarrel therefore that God had with his church, it was for their holding unwarrantable communion with others. The

---

5. John Gill, *Commentary on the Bible,* EWord Today, http://www.ewordtoday.com/comments/genesis/gill/genesis6.htm, accessed 1/10/2012.

6. Matthew Henry, unabridged *Commentary on the Whole Bible,* Christian Classics Ethereal Library, http://www.ccel.org/ccel/henry/mhc1.Gen.vii.html, accessed 1/10/2012.

church should always "dwell alone, and not be reckoned among the nations" (Numbers 23:9). The church is "a chosen generation, a royal priesthood, an holy nation, a peculiar people" (1 Peter 2:9). Therefore the work of the church of God, is not to fall in with any sinful fellowship, or receive into their communion the ungodly world, but to shew forth the praises and virtues of him who hath called them out from among such communicants into his marvellous light.[7]

This summary of four respected commentators from earlier times shows that the prevailing view among biblical scholars was that the "sons of God" were the descendants of Seth, and the "daughters of men" were the descendants of Cain. These commentators were aware of the alternative explanation, but rejected it.

Summary and Conclusion on Verses 1 and 2

In closing our comments on verses 1 and 2, we can also note the following. The daughters of men were beautiful. Some have suggested that their beauty was due to having only a few generations of mutations. But why should such beauty apply only to the descendants of Cain, and not any of the rest of the population? I would suggest that their beauty might be of a more base kind—that these were young ladies who flaunted their sexuality to entrap those who professed to be worshipers of the Lord. In turn, the supposed worshipers of the Lord should have been looking for something else in a wife other than just her physical attractiveness.

Exposition: Genesis 6:3–12

In the first part of our exposition of Genesis 6, we learned about the background to chapter 6, and how wickedness and godlessness was beginning to increase dramatically. We also surveyed the comments from senior classical evangelical commentators on the first two verses of the chapter, and saw that the consensus of the ancients was that the phrase "sons of God" referred to the descendants of Seth, while the phrase "daughters of men" referred to descendants of Cain.

We had also discussed how the descendants of Seth had begun to "call on the Name of the LORD," as described in Genesis 4:26. Thus, the identity of the "sons of God" as the descendants of Seth is reinforced by the beginning of verse 3.

---

7. John Bunyan, *Genesis: A Commentary* (Leicester, England: J6D Publications, Kindle Edition), Locations 3053–3065, edition 2010.

Prophecy of the Flood

It was not unknown in this early history of the world for God's voice to be heard directly. This makes it all the more remarkable that the pre-Flood population was so wicked, if they knew what the voice of the Lord was like.

Of course, it is equally possible that the people did not recognize that it was God who was speaking. Even if they did recognize it, they deliberately ignored Him.

Nevertheless, the fact that God is referred to as the Lord in this verse underlines that He expected to be worshiped, following the pattern of the descendants of Seth in Genesis 4:26. We can surmise that even this worship was not completely wholehearted. It is unlikely, after all, that Noah was the only descendant of Seth. If Noah had brothers, sisters, uncles, aunts, and cousins, then these people all perished in the Flood. Most of the "sons of God" would have been worshipers of the Lord in "a form of godliness but denying its power" (2 Timothy 3:5).

It is not possible to say exactly how God's words were transmitted. Nevertheless, I think it is safe to assume that His words in verse 3 were available for the whole population to hear and take note of, or, as in the case of the vast majority, who were thus without excuse, to hear and ignore.

> My Spirit shall not strive with man forever, for he is indeed flesh;
> yet his days shall be one hundred and twenty years (Genesis 6:3).

God starts by referring to His Spirit. This reminds us that, right from the beginning of the Bible, God was and is Trinity. It was His Spirit who gave energy to the newly created world (Genesis 1:2). And it was the breath of God that made the dust into a living, breathing man, Adam.

Man, in his sinful state, is at war with God. There is no getting around this fact. In our sins, we are people who hate God, who shake our fists in His face. The relationship between God and the unregenerate man is therefore one of strife. Some versions, like the ESV, translate this verse as referring to God not abiding in man forever. God's presence is even with the unregenerate, because without His presence, every man would be as evil as it is possible to be, and would be at complete enmity with God. It is only through the salvation that God has wrought, which is illustrated so aptly for us through the history of the Flood, that peace with God is possible.

God declares that He will not strive with man forever. This does not mean that the sin of the wicked will be overlooked. Nor are these words a prophecy of a mass turning to God in repentance. Rather, it is the sobering recognition that man's war with God is a hopeless war. Man cannot win. God will have the victory, and His name will be glorified. Either a man's sin will be punished on the Cross of Jesus, the sinner saved and God's name glorified, or the man will die in his sins, be judged, found guilty, and sent to hell for everlasting punishment — and God's name will still be glorified. Man is flesh, so every thought of his heart is wicked and a rebellion against God.

Finally, God tells the people that their days are to be 120 years. Some commentators have suggested that this refers to the age that people on average would now live to. However, this does not seem to tie in with facts. It would be many generations after the Flood before the decaying ages of the population would stabilize, and when they did, they would stabilize at an age less than 120 — that is, 70 years.

Therefore, I think it is more likely that God is giving this announcement exactly 120 years before the coming of the Flood. Therefore, those who were prepared to hear (which amounted to only eight people) had 120 years to prepare.

Why did God make this statement? On one level, we do not really know why God would make such a statement. On a human level, it seems as if God is giving the opportunity for people to repent. God is always merciful to those who will repent. Yet we know, in hindsight, that only eight people were saved from the Flood. Did God know that only eight would be saved? If so, then why would He warn people, and wasn't His warning in vain? But if not, then God is not sovereign — whereas Scripture assures us that He is.

I think that God's statement is, in a sense, reiterating a point that God has always made to us, ever since the first sin. There is always the opportunity for salvation for those who believe. Of course, God had planned everything, and knew beforehand who and how many would be saved. The point is that none but the eight on the ark did repent. So those who perished were without excuse, and had only themselves to blame that they perished in the Flood.

What about Giants?

> There were giants on the earth in those days, and also afterward, when the sons of God came in to the daughters of men and they bore children to them. Those were the mighty men who were of old, men of renown (Genesis 6:4).

We have discussed who the sons of God and daughters of men were in a previous chapter, so we will not repeat that discussion here. What is more pertinent at this point is what is meant by the giants.

We should note that the giants were not necessarily offspring of the sons of God and daughters of men, though they could have been. We are simply told that there were giants at the time of the sin that involved the sons of God and daughters of men. We should also be careful with our use of the term "giants." It probably does refer to a preponderance of giantism, but not necessarily. The Hebrew word is *nephilim*. It is possible that super-tall people are being referred to, but it is also possible that this term is simply referring to giantism before the Flood.

When I lived in South Wales, my garden quickly became overrun with a pernicious weed called horsetail. These little fern-like plants grew about six inches high and were very difficult to remove from the lawn. If I traveled just three hours west, I would come to the Pembrokeshire coast, where it was common to find fossilized horsetails. However, the fossils were slightly different from the live ones, because they were not six inches tall, but six feet. They are not the only example of fossils bearing a close resemblance to modern organisms that are a fraction of the size. For example, we know about fossil dragonflies with enormous wingspans. Perhaps it is this giantism that is being referred to by *nephilim* — a giantism that must have been very common before the Flood, but was not unknown after the Flood.

In Numbers 13, we read about the Israelite spies, who went into the Promised Land to report back on whether the land could be conquered. One of the things that so scared 10 of the 12 spies was that they thought some of the people looked like giants, or *nephilim*. They were clearly concerned (due to lack of faith) with the likely outcome of their performance against these giants in battle, but there was more. Look what they got hold of in Numbers 13:23.

> Then they came to the Valley of Eshcol, and there cut down a branch with one cluster of grapes; they carried it between two of them on a pole.

How many clusters of grapes were there? Just one! How did they carry it? Two people had to carry it on a pole. This was a big bunch of grapes, if ever I heard of one! So this was giantism among plant life, and it occurred after the Flood. This is suggested by the following verse in Genesis 6:

There were giants on the earth in those days, *and also afterward* . . . (Genesis 6:4, emphasis added).

Nevertheless, there must have been something a bit special about the offspring of the unholy union. These children were "the mighty men who were of old, men of renown" (Genesis 6:4). They may possibly include some of the characters of legend who are said to possess heroic or godlike qualities. One can certainly suppose that if such people had greater than average strength or abilities, as well as height, they might well have commanded the loyalty, fealty, and even worship of so-called lesser people.

Wickedness Before the Flood

Then the LORD saw that the wickedness of man was great in the earth, and that every intent of the thoughts of his heart was only evil continually (Genesis 6:5).

The phrase "then the LORD saw" does not imply that He was not able to see humanity's sins beforehand, nor that He was impotent to do anything. The verse simply indicates that at this point God turned His attention to this particular problem. "The wickedness of man was great." The Hebrew word for "great" here is *rab*, which indicates an event of major importance. This suggests that mankind's wickedness in the time a hundred years or so before the Flood was a wickedness of enormous significance. We know that people are wicked, but the context suggests that the general wickedness before the Flood was greatly out of the ordinary.

The question we need to ask at this juncture is this: was the special wickedness that was occurring before the Flood much worse than the wickedness that we have today? In order to answer that question, we need to answer this question: why was the wickedness before the Flood so especially heinous to God?

This verse says "every intent of the thoughts of his heart was only evil continually." The problem had to do with the motivation of each individual person in the pre-Flood world. These were people who should have known better. Because of their longevity, in spite of the year being A.M. 1545 (Anno Mundi, the "year of the world," years since creation), there would not have been many generations since the creation. Adam, for example, died in A.M. 930, but Noah's grandfather, Methusaleh, was born in A.M. 687. It is therefore possible that Methusaleh, as a direct descendant in the promised line, might have conversed with Adam, and surely Methusaleh conversed with

Noah, so there was only one generation removed between the creation and the Flood. We have also stated that there were people around — notably descendants of Seth — who were worshiping the Lord, at least in name, if not in reality. Therefore, these people knew what God had done for them, and somehow had access to His voice, since He was able to address the people in verse 3, so there was no excuse for their rebellion and lawlessness. Let us reiterate — they had the clear knowledge of where they had come from, and whose air it was they were breathing, and they had the word of the Lord, and still every intent of their heart was evil.

How does that compare with today? Romans 1:18–23 tells us this:

> For the wrath of God is revealed from heaven against all ungodliness and unrighteousness of men, who suppress the truth in unrighteousness, because what may be known of God is manifest in them, for God has shown it to them. For since the creation of the world His invisible attributes are clearly seen, being understood by the things that are made, even His eternal power and Godhead, so that they are without excuse, because, although they knew God, they did not glorify Him as God, nor were thankful, but became futile in their thoughts, and their foolish hearts were darkened. Professing to be wise, they became fools, and changed the glory of the incorruptible God into an image made like corruptible man — and birds and four-footed animals and creeping things.

Let's repeat a key phrase of that passage, just to make sure it sinks in. "What may be known of God is manifest in them, for God has shown it to them."

"What may be known of God. . . ." What sort of things do you think it is possible to know about God? Is it possible for people to know that He is the Creator? Is it possible to know that He exists and is almighty? Is it possible to know that He is angry and wrathful against sin and the sinners, and that He is also merciful, because He sent His Son to die for sinners? There are some who say that there are people who don't know this, because they weren't brought up that way, and they have never heard. The Bible, in Romans 1, is clearly saying that all these things can be known about God, and therefore they are known, and manifest within people, because "God has shown them." This is a remarkable statement. Noted evolutionist Richard Dawkins knows about God and knows that He is the Almighty Creator, because God has shown him that. God's invisible attributes are no mystery — they are "clearly seen." Just because something is invisible does not make it unknown. So everyone today actually knows about God, but they do not acknowledge Him. Does this sound like the people before the Flood? But wait, the people before the Flood heard the voice of God. Nevertheless, several of them refused to recognize Him. We have seen that in the godless reactions of Lamech, the great-grandson of Cain (not the father of Noah). Today, however, we have something even better. We have the complete written works of God, bound together in a book called the Bible! Whenever we don't know something that God taught, we can look it up. In today's Internet age there are wonderful tools, some freely available on the Internet, for us to search through God's Word and find what we need. So, like the pre-Flood people, today's population knows everything that they need to know about God, and they have His words readily available, yet still their every intent is wicked. Do you not believe that last point? Jeremiah said, "The heart is deceitful above all things, and desperately wicked" (Jeremiah 17:9). The passage does not tell us that the heart was desperately wicked before the Flood but now! It says of our status now that the heart is desperately wicked.

The status of people now is therefore no different than it was before the Flood. The wickedness around today is not less wicked than it was before the Flood. Time and again, the Bible has compared the judgment of the Flood to the judgment to come. Jesus did so in Matthew 24.

> But as the days of Noah were, so also will the coming of the Son of Man be. For as in the days before the flood, they were eating and drinking, marrying and giving in marriage, until the day that Noah entered the ark, and did not know until the flood came and took them all away, so also will the coming of the Son of Man be (Matthew 24:37–39).

Peter made the comparison in 2 Peter 3, reminding us that when scoffers scoff at the idea of a coming judgment, we should remember that God once destroyed the world in a judgment of water, and will destroy it again in a judgment of fire. It therefore follows that the warnings that God gave about a genuine judgment to come before the Flood should give us cause to heed His warnings about a genuine judgment to come, when He returns.

Does God Repent?

> And the LORD was sorry that He had made man on the earth, and He was grieved in His heart (Genesis 6:6)

This is a very sobering verse, and can be difficult to make complete sense of. In the KJV, it reads:

> And it repented the LORD that he had made man on the earth, and it grieved him at his heart.

Does this imply that God has changed His mind over something? Could God really repent of an action? In fact, the KJV translators were very careful in their translation. The verse does not say, "God repented that He had made man on the earth." It says that "it repented the Lord." This is a different kind of statement. It is the equivalent of what the NKJV says, when it reports that "the Lord was sorry that He had made man on the earth."

The fact that this verse cannot be made to imply that God repents and changes his mind is found in 1 Samuel 15:29.

> And also the Strength of Israel will not lie nor repent: for he is not a man, that he should repent (KJV).

This verse is clearly reminding us that God does not change His mind over what He has done. So Genesis 6:6 must mean something else. What the verse is doing is giving us an insight into the emotions felt by God about the situation. God is grieved to the point of pain. God is wounded that those on whom He has poured such love and mercy reject His love and mercy and have chosen wrath for themselves. John Bunyan says:

> Repentance is in us a change of the mind; but in God, a change of his dispensations; for otherwise he repenteth not, neither can he; because it standeth not with the perfection of his nature: In him "is no variableness, neither shadow of turning" (James 1:17). Where-fore, it is man, not God, that turns. When men therefore reject the mercy and ways of God, they cast themselves under his wrath and displeasure; which because it is executed according to the nature of his justice, and the severity of his law, they miss of the mercy promised before (Numbers 23:19). Which that we may know, those shall one day feel that shall continue in final impenitency. There-fore, God speaking to their capacity, he tells them, he hath repented of doing them good. "The Lord repented that he had made Saul king" (1 Samuel 15:35). And yet this repentance was only a change of the dispensation, which Saul by his wickedness had put himself

under; otherwise the strength, the eternity of Israel, "will not lie nor repent" (v. 29).[8]

That is why God could also say, in verse 7, that He had made the beasts and the birds — not that the beasts and the birds had displeased Him, because that is not within their capabilities, but because their presence on the earth sustained the human race, which was now an enemy of God. Romans 5:10 reminds us:

> For if when we were enemies we were reconciled to God through the death of His Son, much more, having been reconciled, we shall be saved by His life.

Saved by Grace

A final reason for these negative comments about the human race, and the whole world, that God had made, is to mark the important contrast with Genesis 6:8.

> But Noah found grace in the eyes of the LORD.

This is such an important verse, that I am going to devote an entire chapter to it at the end of the book. For the moment, let us make a few pertinent comments.

Noah was not saved because he was a man of perfect behavior. Some of his behavior after the Flood demonstrated that. Noah was not even saved because of perfect faith — though it is clear that he was a man of faith. Noah was saved because he found grace in the eyes of the Lord. It has been rightly said that mercy is not receiving what we deserve, whereas grace is receiving what we don't deserve! Noah was saved from the watery judgment of God because of grace. This is precisely the means of salvation today. As the Apostle Paul said:

> For by grace you have been saved through faith, and that not of yourselves; it is the gift of God, not of works, lest anyone should boast (Ephesians 2:8–9).

It is a beautiful thought that Noah was saved "in the eyes of the Lord." We know that we are not righteous. God is not fooled. He knows that we are not righteous. But, following our repentance, we are righteous "in the eyes of the Lord." This is God's decision, to see us as righteous before Him.

---

8. John Bunyan (ed. Paul Taylor, 2010), *Genesis: A Commentary* (Leicester, J6D Publications), Kindle Locations 3165–3174.

Summary and Conclusion

Genesis 6:9–12 forms a neat summary of the situation as it stood before the Flood. Genesis 9 begins with this statement:

> This is the genealogy of Noah.

This statement probably concludes a section of the Book of Genesis that was compiled by Noah. There are a number of such sections in Genesis. For example, Adam's section probably concludes with the opening statement of Genesis 5. So, in my opinion, Genesis 6:9a is the last statement of the section written by Noah, while Genesis 6:9b is the first statement of the section jointly written by Noah's sons, Shem, Ham, and Japheth (Genesis 10:1a). I have written about this division of Genesis into *toledoths* before,[9] accepting the comments of Henry Morris.[10] Along with the late Dr. Morris, I need to emphasize that this acceptance of the idea of separately written *toledoths* (which is the word translated as *generations*) in no way undermines the concept of Moses being the author of Genesis. Henry Morris says:

> It is suggested . . . [in his book *The Genesis Record*] that Moses compiled and edited earlier written records that had been handed down from father to son via the line of the patriarchs listed in Genesis. . . . [Moses] then selected those that were relevant to his own purpose (as guided by the Holy Spirit), added his own explanatory editorial comments and transitional sections, and finally compiled them into the form now known as the Book of Genesis.[11]

If Genesis 6:9a neatly concludes the preceding section, then Genesis 6:9b is a worthy introduction to the new section, in which Noah's sons give a moving testimony to their father.

> Noah was a just man, perfect in his generations. Noah walked with God.

It is a lovely testimony to someone to describe them as "just." How many sons can describe their fathers as "just"? Perhaps a more sobering way of putting it is this — if my sons were writing my biography, would they describe me as a "just" man?

---

9.   Paul F. Taylor, *The Six Days of Genesis* (Green Forest, AR: Master Books, 2007), p. 83–84.
10.   Henry Morris, *The Genesis Record* (Grand Rapids, MI: Baker Book House, 1976), p. 26–30, and 152.
11.   Ibid., p. 26–27.

It is also noteworthy that Noah is described as "perfect in his generations." He was a good man for his times. We know that no one except Christ is absolutely perfect. We also know that perfection is not the means of salvation. But we have also just seen that Noah was not saved by his perfect behavior, but by the grace of God. The fact that he was a good man in evil times was part of his act of worship to God. His good works, therefore, are seen in their proper context, and he was a genuinely good man. Indeed, the Bible later tells us that Noah was one of the three most righteous men in history, along with Daniel and Job (Ezekiel 14:14 and 20). The reason Noah was so righteous was because he took his faith seriously. We read that he "walked with God" — which is, again, one of the most telling tributes that could be paid.

Verses 11 and 12 neatly sum up the problem of the times. Sin is corruption. The word "corrupt" is used three times in these two verses. Corruption implies decay. Sin is being described as something disgusting, like a smelly abscess on the tooth, or a festering, infected wound. There is a tendency today to excuse sin, and minimize the sinfulness of sin. It needs to be seen as something that corrupts, and that spreads, like a nasty disease.

When the Scripture says that "the earth also was corrupt before God," two things are being implied. The population of the earth is being referred to euphemistically as "the earth." However, we can also surmise that the state of the planet itself was affected by sin. The fact that the earth was filled with violence probably refers primarily to the violence of human against human. However, it probably also includes the fact that some animals, though created perfect and vegetarian, were now monsters and carnivores, eating meat and killing in seemingly senseless violence in order to do so. The pre-Flood world was a terrible place. The sobering thought is that today's world is at least equally terrible, corrupt, and violent.

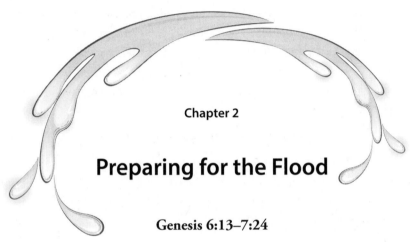

Chapter 2

Preparing for the Flood

Genesis 6:13–7:24

Jesus said:

> But as the days of Noah were, so also will the coming of the Son of Man be. For as in the days before the flood, they were eating and drinking, marrying and giving in marriage, until the day that Noah entered the ark, and did not know until the flood came and took them all away, so also will the coming of the Son of Man be (Matthew 24:37–39).

Jesus' words help us to understand the importance of the historical account of the Flood to our understanding of the gospel — and particularly the importance of the preparation for the Flood. He told us that His return to this earth will be of a similar manner to the coming of the Flood. This makes the preparation for the Flood something like our preparation for Jesus' Second Coming.

Jesus starts by referring to the days of Noah. He would not have used these words if He did not believe that the days of Noah were real. It is also clear that He believed Noah was a real person. Jesus was trying to convince His followers that He was definitely coming again. The force of the argument would be diminished if it were clear that Jesus did not believe that the account of Noah and the Flood was true.

When Jesus says that the people did not know "until the Flood came," it does not mean that they were not aware that God was going to send judgment. It means that they did not believe and therefore were not looking for the judgment to happen when it did. In the same way, our current generation has all the information necessary to let them know that Jesus is coming back and that there will be a future judgment. Nevertheless, because of unbelief, Jesus' return will catch people off guard, and His coming will be like a "thief in the night" (1 Thessalonians 5:2). Note that Jesus emphasizes the judgmental aspect of the Flood — that everyone who was not on the ark was taken away.

It is in this light that we must understand the preparations for the Flood made by Noah — and for that matter, the lack of preparations made by other people.

Building the Ark in a Pre-Flood World

Our chapter "The Design of the Ark" details how the ark was put together and looks at the significance of each part. In this chapter, we will confine ourselves to the spiritual and cultural meanings of the historical account and explain how this is not only a historical account but also speaks to us today.

> And God said to Noah, "The end of all flesh has come before
> Me, for the earth is filled with violence through them; and behold,
> I will destroy them with the earth" (Genesis 6:13).

In Genesis 4, we have an account of God speaking directly to Cain, as He had to Adam. Then we have no record of God speaking directly, until Genesis 6, when He announces the Flood and the time scales in Genesis 6:3, speaking again in Genesis 6:7. We are not told to whom God was speaking on those occasions. It is possible that He was speaking through a prophet, such as Noah himself, or maybe his great-grandfather Enoch. It is also possible that, somehow, God made His words directly known to the entire human population, even though they did not accept His message. I suspect, though I cannot prove, that verses 3 and 7 were delivered to Noah, whose responsibility was to proclaim that message widely. This is because God usually speaks through human prophets, and Noah was the most obvious person at the time for the prophecy to be delivered to, as it directly concerned his faith and obedience.

So in verse 13 we have God (once again) speaking to Noah. God starts by explaining to Noah about the judgment to come and the reason for it.

Why does God give the reason for the Flood, as well as tell Noah what He was going to do? Part of the answer to that question must be to do with the grace that God showed Noah (Genesis 6:8). This is in line with God telling Abraham about the coming destruction of Sodom and Gomorrah.

> And the LORD said, "Shall I hide from Abraham what I am doing, since Abraham shall surely become a great and mighty nation, and all the nations of the earth shall be blessed in him? For I have known him, in order that he may command his children and his household after him, that they keep the way of the LORD, to do righteousness and justice, that the LORD may bring to Abraham what He has spoken to him" (Genesis 18:17–19).

Another reason why God may have told Noah about His plans was so that He could tell others. The New Testament tells us that Noah was a "preacher of righteousness."

> [God] did not spare the ancient world, but saved Noah, one of eight people, a preacher of righteousness, bringing in the flood on the world of the ungodly (2 Peter 2:5).

To see how this preaching worked in practice, we must remind ourselves of the time scales involved. If Genesis 6:3 is announcing the Flood, then this announcement occurred in approximately A.M. 1536 (*Anno Mundi*, the year of the world — i.e., after creation). The only two patriarchs in the promised lineage who were still alive, other than Noah himself, were Noah's father and grandfather, Lamech and Methusaleh. Perhaps it is not too much speculation to suggest that their names indicate different approaches to the Flood. Methusaleh (some say may mean "his death shall bring") represents faith in God, whereas Lamech ("weary") represents either unbelief or a stoic acceptance of judgment with no hope.

The Faith of Noah

It is clear that Noah accepted the clear instruction from God. Calvin says:

> For it was necessary, that in utter despair of help from any other quarter, he should seek his safety, by faith, in the ark. For so long as life was promised to him on earth, never would he have been so intent as he ought, in the building of the ark; but, being alarmed by the judgment of God, he earnestly embraces the promise of life

given unto him. He no longer relies upon the natural causes or means of life; but rests exclusively on the covenant of God, by which he was to be miraculously preserved. No labor is now troublesome or difficult to him; nor is he broken down by long fatigue. For the spur of God's anger pierces him too sharply to allow him to sleep in carnal delights, or to faint under temptations, or to be delayed in his course by vain hope: he rather stirs himself up, both to flee from sin, and to seek a remedy.[1]

The New Testament reminds us of Noah's faithfulness in this matter.

> By faith Noah, being divinely warned of things not yet seen, moved with godly fear, prepared an ark for the saving of his household, by which he condemned the world and became heir of the righteousness which is according to faith (Hebrews 11:7).

Calvin referred to this verse when he noted that Noah acted out of "godly fear." Godly fear is not about being terrified, but about having the proper respect for the awesomeness and authority of God. Noah had this, because he was warned about the Flood by God. He therefore did what God commanded. It was for this reason that the rest of the world was condemned. On a human level, the other people in the world could have been saved, but they would not. So, when they stand before the Judgment Seat of God, they will be without excuse, because Noah, that preacher of righteousness, told them long ago what would happen if they did not repent.

Noah had 120 years to build his ark. This was plenty of time for the project, though it is possible that he could have had others to help him, apart from his sons. It is possible that people close to Noah, and even involved with the ark's construction, simply refused to believe, and so ended up missing history's most important boat trip. It could have been these close associates, to whom Noah was preaching.

The substance of God's message of judgment was this: Everything that had the life of the flesh was to die. This was because "the earth was filled with violence." This violence is indicative of major sins against the peace and holiness of godly living. God's statements leave no room for doubt. He intends to bring the world to an end and save only that which is saved by faith.

Verses 14 through 16 outline important aspects about the construction of the ark that we have already studied. It may be worth remembering at this

---

1. John Calvin, *Commentary on Genesis*, Christian Classics Ethereal Library, http://www.ccel. org/ccel/calvin/calcom01.xii.i.html, accessed 2/21/2012.

point that the word "pitch" is really the Hebrew word for "covering," used elsewhere in the Old Testament for "atonement." Thus it is emphasized to us that the ark was a means of salvation, and, as such, is a type of Christ. Peter makes this point in his first epistle.

> For Christ also suffered once for sins, the just for the unjust, that He might bring us to God, being put to death in the flesh but made alive by the Spirit, by whom also He went and preached to the spirits in prison, who formerly were disobedient, when once the Divine longsuffering waited in the days of Noah, while the ark was being prepared, in which a few, that is, eight souls, were saved through water (1 Peter 3:18–20).

Matthew Henry, commenting on 1 Peter, remarks that the spirits were not in prison when Jesus preached to them, but that was their destination, because they failed to repent.

> Because they were dead and disembodied when the apostle speaks of them, therefore he properly calls them spirits now *in prison;* not that they were *in prison when Christ preached to them,* as the vulgar Latin translation and the popish expositors pretend. . . . They were *disobedient,* that is, *rebellious, unpersuadable,* and *unbelieving,* as the word signifies; this their sin is aggravated from the patience and *long-suffering of God* (which *once waited* upon them for 120 years together), *while Noah was preparing the ark,* and by that, as well as by his preaching, giving them fair warning of what was coming upon them.[2]

In verse 17, God tells Noah how He will destroy the earth, that He will do it by floodwaters.

> And behold, I Myself am bringing floodwaters on the earth, to destroy from under heaven all flesh in which is the breath of life; everything that is on the earth shall die (Genesis 6:17).

The use of "I Myself" serves to underline the import of what God is telling Noah. He then goes on to specify which animals are going to die. It is going to be those "in which is the breath of life." This explains why Noah had to save two of every kind of land vertebrate that breathes with lungs as well as birds and other flying vertebrates. Invertebrates that do not breathe

---

2. Matthew Henry, *Commentary on the Whole Bible,* Christian Classics Ethereal Library, http://www.ccel.org/ccel/henry/mhc6.iPet.iv.html, accessed 2/21/2012, emphasis added.

with lungs would not need to be on the ark. So Noah did not have to take two woodworms on the ark! Invertebrates can often survive modern floods, whether dormant or rafting on uprooted vegetation.

Then we come to the most significant salvation verse since Genesis 6:8:

> But I will establish My covenant with you; and you shall go into the ark — you, your sons, your wife, and your sons' wives with you (Genesis 6:18).

God made a covenant with Noah. What was Noah's side of the covenant? Simply to believe. Noah could do nothing to stem the floodwaters. He was not expected to participate as an equal partner in this covenant at all. Noah was simply given the means of salvation, and the only part he played, if you could call it that, was to act in the obedience that comes from faith. As Paul says:

> For by grace you have been saved through faith, and that not of yourselves; it is the gift of God, not of works, lest anyone should boast (Ephesians 2:8–9).

Noah was not even saved by his work in building the ark; that was simply his act of obedience stemming from his faith. He was saved by grace alone, through faith.

Following this, we have more instructions that we discuss in the chapter "The Design of the Ark." Genesis 6 then ends with a statement that should be true of anyone who puts his or her trust in the Lord.

> Thus Noah did; according to all that God commanded him, so he did (Genesis 6:22).

Following the commandments of God is never optional. It is our duty. While we are not saved by our works — this is hammered home throughout the New Testament — our works flowing from our faith are the clear indication to the world that we are saved. Noah's obedience in building an ark was a clear testimony to the doubters around him. When the feet of the doubters began to get wet, they would know that they were without excuse.

Entering the Ark

> Then the LORD said to Noah, "Come into the ark, you and all your household, because I have seen that you are righteous before Me in this generation" (Genesis 7:1).

God said to Noah, "Come into the ark," not "Go into the ark." This is because God was in the ark already, because He had ordained it as our means of salvation. Typology, like metaphor, must not be pushed too hard, and obviously the ark was not God, but this language reminds us that God invites us to salvation, through Jesus, and this very invitation is only possible because Jesus was and is God. We see again that Noah was invited in because he was righteous. We have studied earlier that this righteousness is the righteousness that comes by faith, rather than a vain attempt to be as good as humanly possible. The best that is humanly possible is not good enough for God. Noah's righteousness was "before Me [God]." It is not too difficult for a man to appear righteous before his peers and even before the world at large. However, Noah was righteous before God, who sees everything. It is God, not people, whom we should be seeking to please. Noah's righteousness was "in this generation." This indicates how rare Noah's righteousness was — in fact, unique. It also reminds us that Noah's whole demeanor was a witness and a sermon to those around him.

Even after Noah and his family had entered the ark, God waited another seven days before sending the Flood. On one level, this shows more about the mercy of God. Humanly speaking, it was still possible, once the ark was complete, for some people to repent and come on board the ark for salvation. Yet God knew that no one else would come. Does this mean that the seven days was a failure or a sham? Not at all! God also knew that after the Flood there would be those who might want to point an accusing finger at God — that He had not provided enough time for salvation; as if 120 years were not enough. So God made absolutely sure that there was no possibility of anyone offering an excuse. There was none. And in seven days, the floodwaters did indeed come, just as God had said they would.

One of the most significant verses in the account of the Flood is Genesis 7:16:

> So those that entered, male and female of all flesh, went in as God had commanded him; and the LORD shut him in.

There is another reminder that Noah was being obedient in his actions, but it is in the last part of the verse, which is so often overlooked. The ark contained a door — only one door. But Noah did not close the door. It was God who closed the door. This reminds us that our salvation has everything to do with God and nothing to do with us. Jesus said:

I am the door. If anyone enters by Me, he will be saved, and will
go in and out and find pasture (John 10:9).

This is how close an analogy there is between the ark and the saving
work of Jesus. Jesus is the door, and it is only through Him that we can be
saved. The work is accomplished solely through Him. In the same way, it
was the Lord who shut the door of the ark, to make sure that Noah and his
family were safe.

All Flesh Died

The waters prevailed fifteen cubits upward, and the mountains
were covered. And all flesh died that moved on the earth: birds and
cattle and beasts and every creeping thing that creeps on the earth,
and every man. All in whose nostrils was the breath of the spirit of
life, all that was on the dry land, died. So He destroyed all living
things which were on the face of the ground: both man and cattle,
creeping thing and bird of the air. They were destroyed from the
earth. Only Noah and those who were with him in the ark remained
alive. And the waters prevailed on the earth one hundred and fifty
days (Genesis 7:20–24).

There are those who claim to have a high view of Scripture, yet will not
believe that the Flood was a real, global event. Many claim that it can be
interpreted as a local event, without doing damage to their belief in the inerrancy of Scripture. But their position will simply not do. The Bible clearly
teaches that "all flesh died that moved on the earth." The Bible lists the three
categories of land animals, and the birds (or *fowl*, as the KJV has it, with a
better translation of the Hebrew *ôph*). Once again, it is emphasized that it
was the animals that could breathe that died, and therefore whose represen-
tatives were saved on the ark.

God means what He says. He has pronounced judgment on sin. That
judgment will be carried out. God did it once before, at the time of the
Flood. No one should dare believe that He will not do it again.

Chapter 3

God Remembered Noah

Genesis 8:1–19

Could God have forgotten Noah? Why is it so significant that He remembered Noah? What sort of a God is He, if He could forget someone? Could the ark have been left floating the vast planet-wide ocean, if God hadn't suddenly remembered Noah?

Of course, these questions fundamentally misunderstand the nature of God. God will never forget His people.

> He will not forsake you nor destroy you, nor forget the covenant of your fathers which He swore to them (Deuteronomy 4:31).

God does not forget the covenants that He has made. We are the ones who forget these covenants.

> Take heed to yourselves, lest you forget the covenant of the LORD your God which He made with you, and make for yourselves a carved image in the form of anything which the LORD your God has forbidden you (Deuteronomy 4:23).

There is something that God does not remember, however.

> For I will be merciful to their unrighteousness, and their sins and their lawless deeds I will remember no more (Hebrews 8:12).

Notice that even here, God is not forgetful. The fact that He chooses to remember our sins no more is a deliberate act of will on His part.

But this is to stray off the subject. God had made a covenant with Noah. He was not going to forget Noah. So why does the Scripture say that He remembered Noah? It is because this was an ongoing remembrance of Noah. He called Noah to remembrance constantly. He never left Noah to drift aimlessly. Noah and the ark were always part of God's active plan, which He brought to fruition perfectly.

God Is Active

What we are really learning in Genesis 8:1 is that God is active. Theistic evolutionists believe that God has created this world by a process of blind evolution. Although they object strongly when I say it, they basically believe that God has set everything going and then stands back in order to observe it, without real involvement. Genesis 8:1 is, therefore, strong evidence against theistic evolution. God left nothing to chance. He brought Noah to His remembrance, and also every living thing, every animal that was with Noah on the ark. Whether or not the wind that God sent was responsible for causing the the waters to subside is a matter of conjecture. The verse does not necessarily have to be interpreted in that way. It could simply be two factors occurring together. God made the waters subside and He sent a wind. However, what God definitely did at this point was stop the volcanic and seismic activity of the "fountains of the deep." If the CTP model, outlined in the chapter on how the Flood started, is correct, then the miraculous closing of the "fountains of the deep" would also have closed the "windows of heaven."

Where did the waters go? Genesis 8 does not make this clear, but fortunately another passage of Scripture can help. In Psalm 104:5–9 we read this:

> You who laid the foundations of the earth, so that it should not
> be moved forever, You covered it with the deep as with a garment;
> the waters stood above the mountains. At Your rebuke they fled; at
> the voice of Your thunder they hastened away. They went up over
> the mountains; they went down into the valleys, to the place which
> You founded for them. You have set a boundary that they may not
> pass over, that they may not return to cover the earth.

An alternative rendering of Psalm 104:8 reads as follows:

> The mountains rose; the valleys sank down.

This alternative reading is the one used in the NASB and the ESV. It is odd that this is not the major reading in the KJV and NKJV, because this rendering seems to be the one available in the Masoretic Text, according to Charles Taylor. Dr. Taylor used the figure below in order to help understand where the two alternative readings came from.

Hebrew	עָלָה	הַר	יָרַד	בִּקְעָה
Romanised	ʿâlâh	har	yârad	biqʿâh
English	Rise	Mountains	Sink	Valleys

Taylor concludes thus:

> We notice that verse 7 of Psalm 104 has already told us that the waters "fled," so why would they then go up again over the mountains? The flow of the narrative indicates that in verse 8 we have a new feature, in which our attention is drawn to the mountains and valleys themselves, but with the waters and their bounds still in mind. Then in verse 9 our attention is once more given to the waters, to which the mountains and valleys, and indeed the land in general, formed a barrier, so that the waters would never again flood the whole Earth. That seems the most reasonable understanding of the passage as a whole.[1]

This rendering makes sense and is in accord with the Hebrew. Taylor also notes that the LXX Greek translation of the Old Testament very definitely puts the words "mountains" and "valleys" in the nominative case, thus making them the subjects of their clauses, rather than the indirect objects.

Although God had stopped the volcanic/seismic activity associated with the "fountains of the deep," this ESV/NASB rendering suggests that mountain ranges became higher and ocean trenches ("valleys") became lower. Thus, between these two effects, all the Floodwater could be contained. Deep sea diver and broadcaster Jacques Cousteau once said:

> Were the crust of Earth to be leveled — with great mountain ranges like the Himalayas and ocean abysses like the Mariana Trench evened out — no land at all would show above the surface of the

---

1. Charles Taylor, "Did Mountains Really Rise According to Psalm 104:8?" *CEN Technical Journal* 12 (3) 1998, also available at http://creation.com/images/pdfs/tj/j12_3/j12_3_312-313.pdf, accessed 2/22/2012.

sea. Earth would be covered by a uniform sheet of water — more than 10,000 feet deep! So overwhelming the ocean seems to be.[2]

CPT theory makes sense of this. Traditional uniformitarian plate tectonics does not make sense of the formation of the Himalayas, for example. Slow movement of the Indian-Australian plate colliding at very low velocity with the Asian plate would not seem to produce the sort of catastrophic effect needed for this huge mountain range. However, if the Indian-Australian and Asian plates collided rapidly during the Flood, while still submerged, we can see how such a giant range of mountains could be produced.

The Ark on Ararat

Perhaps a word needs to be said about the "discovery" of ark fragments in the region of Ararat. Genesis 8:4 does not say that the ark landed on top of Mount Ararat. Instead, the implication is that the ark landed somewhere in the region.

The recent history of creation science appears to be littered with examples of people claiming to have found the ark. As I write this chapter, a new story is unfolding, with many keen creationist advocates and others urging caution.

I have to confess that I am one of those that urge caution. I am a skeptical creationist. I believe that creationism is damaged by the many false starts in this area. Of course, I would be as fascinated as the next creationist if the ark really did turn up. However, I have grave doubts. It is my strong opinion that the ark will never be found, and that any remains of the ark disintegrated long ago. This statement tends to offend those who have invested emotional capital in one of the many ark claims. However, I will say again, I think it is very, very unlikely that anyone will find remnants of the ark in the region of Ararat. What if they did? What is the best evidence that the ark actually existed? It is not the finding of a relic in eastern Turkey. The best evidence that the ark existed is the documentary evidence that we have in the Book of Genesis. Don't get me wrong — if someone actually finds something genuine there, I will be as excited as the next man, but I am not looking to such finds to validate the Bible. Whenever we attempt to use evidences of this kind to validate the Bible, we are actually setting up the evidences as higher authority than the Bible, and that is something we should never do.

---

2. Jacques Cousteau, *The Ocean World of Jacques Cousteau — Oasis in Space* (London, England: Angus & Robertson Ltd., 1973), p.17.

The Ark Rested

The idea that the ark "rested," as stated in Genesis 8:4, is an interesting word choice. This episode of the Flood account is rich in typology. Readers will recall that a type is like a sort of living metaphor. For example, if the ark was a metaphor of Christ, then the ark would not be real but merely a figure of speech. However, when we say that the ark is a *type* of Christ, we mean that it was a genuine object, and that it speaks to us figuratively about Christ as well. So, as I discuss the figurative meanings of some of these events in Genesis 8, I am looking at types, not metaphors. In other words, nothing that I state should be taken to imply that I don't think the account is historically factual. On the contrary, it is both factual and it speaks to us figuratively.

When the ark came to rest, it was the 17th day of the seventh month. Jesus rose from the dead on the 17th day of the second month. However, the religious calendar took on a new numbering of months at the time of the Passover. Henry Morris points out:

> The seventh month of the Jewish civil year (and this is proba-
> bly the calendar used here in Genesis 7 and 8) later was made the
> first month of the religious year, and the Passover was set for the
> fourteenth day of that month (Exodus 12:2). Christ, our Passover
> (1 Corinthians 5:7), was slain on that day, but then rose three days
> later, on the seventeenth day of the seventh month of the civil
> calendar.[3]

The next weeks must have been difficult for the occupants of the ark. The ark had not landed, and the water was receding. Yet there still had to be more time spent waiting. Here is the time scale:

- month 7, day 7: ark lands

- month 10, day 1, 10 weeks and 4 days after landing: tops of mountains appear

- 40 days later, 16 weeks and 2 days after landing: Noah sends out the raven

- 7 days later, 17 weeks and 2 days after landing: Noah sends out dove

---

3. Henry Morris, *The Genesis Record* (Grand Rapids, MI: Baker Book House, 1976), p. 209.

- 7 days later, 18 weeks and 2 days after landing: Noah sends out dove again

- 7 days later, 19 weeks and 2 days after landing: Noah sends out the dove the third and final time

- month 1, day 1, 23 weeks and 3 days after landing: Noah removes the ark's covering

- month 2, day 27, 31 weeks and 3 days after landing: Noah, his family, and the animals disembark

The disembarkation, therefore, was nearly eight months after the ark had landed. Bunyan comments on the delay in the disembarkation thus:

> Now we are come to the end of the trial, and so to the time of Noah's deliverance, and behold as he went in, so he came out: He went into the ark at the commandment of the Lord. "And the Lord said unto Noah, Come thou and all thy house into the ark" (Gen 7:1). And here again, "And God spake unto Noah, saying, Go forth of the ark." Hence note, that notwithstanding the earth was dry about fifty-four days before, yet Noah waited for the word of God for his commission to bring him forth of the ark. Providence seemed to smile before, in that the earth was dry, to which had but Noah added reason, he must have concluded, the time is come for me to go forth of the ark. But Noah knew, that as well the providences of God, as the waters of the flood might be to try his dependence on the word of the Lord: wherefore, though he saw this, yet because he had no answer of God, he will not take the opportunity.[4]

When Noah first saw land, he must have been horrified by the devastation he witnessed. The planet was covered with sediment. As the waters abated, there would have been huge seismic activity causing the uplift of mountain ranges. It is possible that Noah would have heard or seen some of this process. As the waters began to recede, he would have witnessed the carving out of canyons and other such features. Finally, hope would have been rekindled, because the ground must have miraculously recovered quickly, and new plants must have germinated quickly. Remember that the Flood was a supernatural event. Those scoffers who maintain that

---

4. John Bunyan (P. Taylor, editor), *Genesis: A Commentary* (Leicester, UK: J6D Publications, 2009, Kindle edition), Kindle Locations 4453–4459.

new vegetation could not have rapidly colonized the post-Flood world are forgetting the power of God.

Covenant with Creation

Some of the greatest men of the Old Testament are those who put the worship of God first. Abel was such a man, sacrificing blood offerings, rather than relying on his own merits. Abraham was such a man, building an altar at the Terebinth tree as one of his first actions in his new land. Noah, likewise, begins his time on the new earth by building an altar. We are not sure if Noah took 7 of each clean animal on the ark or 14 (seven pairs). If it was the smaller number, then, as Noah took one of each clean animal, there were still at least three breeding pairs left to repopulate the world. Even after the sacrifices, the clean animals still had a three-to-one advantage over the unclean animals.

God, in response, makes a covenant with nature. He promises not to "curse the ground for man's sake." Notice that God did not expect everything to be perfect with humanity, now that the Flood had come and gone. He says, "The imagination of man's heart is evil from his youth" (Genesis 8:21). Note that God does not say that this evil-heartedness was in the past, and that He expected Noah's descendants to be good. On the contrary, he expected Noah's descendants to be bad, and to need a Savior.

Then God stated how nature would function.

> While the earth remains,
> Seedtime and harvest,
> Cold and heat,
> Winter and summer,
> And day and night
> Shall not cease (Genesis 8:22).

Today, there are many people worrying about issues such as global warming and climate change. Actually, the whole concept of global warming and climate change is a problematic area, and its doomsayers are false prophets; but that would be a huge bunny trail to make a major comment on that area.[5] For now, we should note that there is nothing that we can do to stop the seasons from occurring, because that is the pattern God set in Genesis 8:22.

---

5. For a biblical perspective on the issue of global warming/climate change, see Jay A. Auxt and William M. Curtis, III, *Global Warming and the Creator's Plan* (Green Forest, AR: Master Books, 2009).

Final Comments

There are some who have said to me that the account of the Flood is proof that God does not allow His saints to go through times of tribulation. Yet, think what Noah and his family endured when they were in the ark. It is true that God saved them from the Flood, and it is true that God actively remembered them and brought them through to the other side. But it is not true to say that there was no suffering involved. God does not promise us an easy ride as Christians, but He does promise to be with us and He does promise to save us. Noah's time in the ark up to his disembarkation is witness to that fact.

Chapter 4

A Covenant and a Rainbow

Genesis 9:1–17

Few things in creation are as beautiful or wonderful as a rainbow. It is a scientific phenomenon that can be expressed in terms of numbers associated with frequencies and wavelengths of light, and it is also an artistic object, enjoyed because of its beauty.

The rainbow is based on some basic principles of physics. Isaac Newton's famous experiment on white light utilized a clear prism — a toblerone-shaped piece of glass or Perspex. White light is shone into the prism at such an angle that it bends toward the normal (vertical). On emergence from the prism, the light bends away from the new normal, but because they are set at a triangle shape, this merely increases the bending, such that there is an

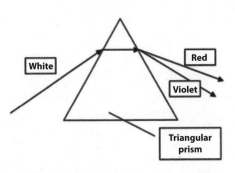

actual observable difference between this bending (or *refraction*) for light of differing frequencies.

Because violet light has the greatest frequency, and hence the shortest wavelength, of visible light, it is bent to a greater angle than red light, at the opposite end of the visible spectrum. The trouble with scientific statements like these is that they sound cold, but the effect of these different refractions for different frequencies is stunningly beautiful.

Have you noticed how rainbows are always opposite the sun? If you are facing the rainbow, then the sun is behind you. A similar refraction happens with spherical raindrops, but in this case, because the internal angles of the light rays are greater than the critical angle of water, the rays undergo *total internal reflection* before they are refracted again as they leave the water drop. Once again, the effect is stunningly

beautiful, as you can see in the photo of a double rainbow.

What a spectacular phenomenon it is, therefore, that God chose to use as a sign of the covenant He made with Noah. In the previous chapter, we looked at the covenant God made concerning nature. Now we look particularly at His first main covenant with a human, and this so-called Noahic Covenant is really a covenant with the whole human race, whether they all realize it or not. For this reason, all the provisions of this Noahic Covenant are still in operation today. It can be referred to as the covenant of common grace, because it is God's commitment to all humanity, whether they serve Him or not. It is a covenant that is designed to set forth the articles of good governance. And we should note that God takes ownership of this covenant — He describes it as "My covenant" (Genesis 9:11) and the sign of the covenant is "My rainbow" (Genesis 9:13).

God Blesses Noah

Chapter 9 starts with God blessing Noah and his sons. He also gives them a commission: "Be fruitful and multiply, and fill the earth." In the KJV, this verse reads "replenish the Earth." Today, the word *replenish* means "to fill again," and one might expect that God was commanding Noah's family to fill the earth again. Therefore, this verse has been compared with Genesis 1:28, which uses the same word, to suggest another flood before the creation week. However, the Hebrew word for fill/replenish is *mâlê* (אלמ), which means to fill completely, not to fill again. Even in English, we find that in 1611 the word *replenish* did not mean "to fill again," but did, in fact, mean "to fill completely." The KJV is the only translation that uses the word replenish. The Geneva Bible has "fill" in 1:28, with "replenish" in 9:1, while Tyndale uses "fill" in both verses. So, God is instructing Noah and his family that they are to fill the earth completely. When we study the Tower of Babel incident, in Genesis 11, we can therefore see the extent of the people's disobedience by their refusal to obey this simple command.

A Changed World

God then gives instructions to Noah that will directly help him in the brand-new environment of the new post-Flood world. The first noticeable change was that of the behavior of animals.

In this new world, God warns Noah that there would now be fear and dread of mankind among animals. This presents us with the tantalizing thought that before the Flood animals may not have been afraid of people. It would seem obvious that, when created, there was no fear at all between man and animal. After the Fall, however, some animals may have begun to eat meat. While this may have caused isolated problems for people, the strong implication of Genesis 9:2 is that animals' fear of people was not widespread before the Flood. In the post-Flood world, however, things would change.

For those who long for a world in which we can cuddle lions, perhaps it ought to be said that the fear animals have for people is to our advantage. One of my favorite old films is Alfred Hitchcock's *The Birds*. The sight of ordinary seabirds taking on a menacing and threatening attitude toward people is truly chilling, and underlines the fact that it is a relief in a changed world of carnivores that birds and animals are actually scared of us.

It is also noteworthy that, of the three groups of land animals given earlier, no mention is made of the *cattle* or *livestock*. Thus, there are domesticated animals that do not fear us, because they depend on us. Evolutionists assume that domestication is something that has evolved. Although there is the possibility of domesticating certain types of animals, it seems to be the case that genuine domestication is something built into the psyche of those animals, for which it is intended.

The second major change of the post-Flood world was to our diet. Genesis 1:29 says:

> And God said, "See, I have given you every herb that yields seed which is on the face of all the earth, and every tree whose fruit yields seed; to you it shall be for food."

So our original diet was intended to be vegetarian. Now it is possible that some people may have started to eat meat before the Flood, because there was really no end to how many of God's laws the pre-Flood people were prepared to break. Nevertheless, pre-Flood burger houses would have been sinful. In the post-Flood world, however, God was giving us permission to eat meat from animals. "Every moving thing that lives shall be food for you," said God (Genesis 9:3), and there are some who would say that certain burger houses do make their products from every moving thing! But I could not possibly comment.

There is always some confusion over verse 4; "But you shall not eat flesh with its life, that is, its blood." Some have used this to suggest that food products made from blood should not be eaten. I am not so sure about this, and suspect that it might refer to not eating animals when they are alive, and is therefore a plea to humane killing of animals. After all, red meat contains blood, but this cannot be excluded from the sort of meat that we may eat. It should be pointed out that, of two great commentators, Calvin would have disagreed with my position,[1] while Matthew Henry takes the same position as I do.

> It was necessary to add this limitation to the grant of liberty to eat flesh, lest, instead of nourishing their bodies by it, they should destroy them. God would hereby show, (1.) That though they were lords of the creatures, yet they were subjects to the Creator, and under the restraints of his law. (2.) That they must not be greedy and hasty in taking their food, but stay the preparing of it; not like Saul's soldiers (1 Sam. xiv. 32), nor *riotous eaters of flesh*, Prov.

---

1. John Calvin, *Commentary on Genesis*, http://www.ccel.org/ccel/calvin/calcom01.xv.i.html, accessed 2/24/2012.

xxiii. 20. (3.) That they must not be barbarous and cruel to the inferior creatures. They must be lords, but not tyrants; they might kill them for their profit, but not torment them for their pleasure, nor tear away the member of a creature while it was yet alive, and eat that. (4.) That during the continuance of the law of sacrifices, in which the blood made *atonement for the soul* (Lev. xvii. 11), signifying that the life of the sacrifice was accepted for the life of the sinner, blood must not be looked upon as a common thing, but must be *poured out before the Lord* (2 Sam. xxiii. 16), either upon his altar or upon his earth. But, now that the great and true sacrifice has been offered, the obligation of the law ceases with the reason of it.[2]

Why would God have made this change in our diet? It is probably because of the ongoing effect of the Fall. Plant protein was presumably enough to nourish us in the early days, but by the time the Flood had ended, plant protein was not sufficient. Therefore, animal protein was permitted in order to keep us healthy. Strict vegans must be careful about getting the right mix of proteins and other supplements in order to supplement for the range of nutrients they would ingest automatically if they ate meat.

Whether Calvin or Henry is correct, it would appear that God is once again underlining the importance of blood, in preparation for the gospel.

This brings us naturally to the third major change in the post-Flood world — that God lays down the natural order of justice for murder.

In the later books of the Pentateuch, we read about national laws that do not always apply directly today. Critics rightly suggest, therefore, that capital punishment for theft or for adultery is no longer appropriate today, even though the existence of such sanctions in the Mosaic laws reminds us about how seriously God takes such sins. However, some have gone further to suggest that capital punishment is never appropriate. For example, it is a rule that no nation in the membership of the European Union may have capital punishment on its statute book. Therefore, though a large majority of British people, for example, would like to see the restoration of capital punishment,[3] it will not be possible, due to the United Kingdom's membership in the European Union.

---

2. Matthew Henry, *Commentary on the Whole Bible*, http://www.ccel.org/ccel/henry/mhc1. Gen.x.html, accessed 2/24/2012.

3. YouGov survey, October 2010, http://cdn.yougov.com/today_uk_import/YG-Archives-Pol-Prospect-SocialMoralIssues_101026.pdf.

As C.S. Lewis pointed out, however, whether a law should be in place or not does not depend on whether or not it has majority support, but on whether or not it is morally right.[4]

For that reason, we should note that God instructed Noah to sentence capital execution for murder, long before the Mosaic laws and covenant. Because the Noahic Covenant is a covenant of common grace, this provision is still in force today, and should be the natural order of things. That an organization like the EU should outlaw capital punishment for murder merely shows how far from biblical truth the EU has gone. In an earlier comment on these verses, I said:

> Many readers who have traveled with me through this book will feel unable to join me in these views. I respect that, but ask that you respect that, for many Christians, our support for the death penalty for murder, which seems so incongruous to many, is based on Genesis 9:6, and not on some misapplication of the Levitical laws. We are, after all, already under the death penalty from God, because of the sin of Genesis 3.[5]

The Covenant Sealed

We started this chapter with some science about rainbows. In verses 8 through 17 we read about the theology of rainbows. Is there a connection between the two? I think that there is.

It is important to remember that we do not really know whether or not there was rain before the Flood. This surprises some people who have taken it as an article of faith that the vapor canopy prevented pre-Flood precipitation. However, in this book we discuss why the canopy theory does not hold water — pun intended! So under the Flood models we have used, there may or may not have been rain before the Flood. Although I do not make it a major stumbling block, my personal view is that there wasn't any rain before the Flood, because raindrops need dust around which to coalesce — dust that is probably best explained as a result of the volcanic activity that caused the Flood.

If I am right, then we would suggest that there were no rainbows before the Flood. Again, this is not an absolutely necessary inference, but it would

4. C.S. Lewis, "The Humanitarian Theory of Punishment," *Issues In Religion And Psychotherapy*, 13(1), 1987, https://ojs.lib.byu.edu/spc/index.php/IssuesInReligionAndPsychotherapy/article/view/273/272, accessed 2/24/2012.

5. Paul F. Taylor, *The Six Days of Genesis* (Green Forest, AR: Master Books, 2007), p. 181.

seem that God's institution of the rainbow as a symbol for this covenant with all people would suggest that it did not exist before this point.

Genesis 9:16 says that God remembers His covenant with us all every time He sees the rainbow. I think that we, too, can take joy in the sight of a rainbow, not just because of its beauty, but because it reminds us that God always keeps His promises.

An important corollary of this fact is that God's faithfulness demands that the Flood had to have been global. How can I justify that claim?

God promised never again to flood the earth. There have been local floods since the Genesis Flood, but none of these have covered the earth. Therefore, God has indeed kept His promise.

But what if you believe that the Genesis Flood was just a local flood? Then there have been lots of devastating floods since the Genesis Flood. If you believe that the Genesis Flood was a local flood, then you have to say that God has not kept His promises.

In November 2009, the county of Cumbria in the northwest of England suffered devastating floods that affected the highways and downtown areas of major towns, like Workington (pictured)[6] and Cockermouth. The BBC news coverage described the flooding as "biblical."[7] Try standing on that now-dry street in Cockermouth and preaching to the people there that God keeps His promises, if you believe that the Genesis Flood was a local flood.

I believe that God always keeps His promises. He has never sent a planet-covering deluge like He did about 1,656 years after creation.

An Imperfect First Family

Nehru said:

> History is almost always written by the victors and conquerors and gives their view.[8]

---

6. Andy V. Byers at en.wikipedia [CC-BY-3.0 (http://creativecommons.org/licenses/by/3.0)], from Wikimedia Commons.

7. http://www.bbc.co.uk/blogs/richardmoss/2010/11/_the_devastating_impact_of.html.

8. Jawaharlal Nehru, *The Discovery of India* (Oxford: Oxford University Press, 1946).

It is assumed by many, implicit in Nehru's statement, that history books will paint the victors in a good light, making them heroes. The Bible does not follow this presupposition, giving a "warts and all" analysis of some of its most important figures. Since the Bible spent several chapters talking about Noah, his faithfulness and obedience, one would have assumed that Noah is a biblical hero. How could the Bible then turn on him and report his failings? The reason it did so is because his failings really did happen. Noah was not superman. He was a man of frailty. Bunyan expresses this surprise at Noah's actions.

> This is the blot in this good man's scutcheon; and a strange blot it is, that such an one as Noah should be thus overtaken with evil! One would have thought that Moses should now have began with a relation of some eminent virtues, and honourable actions of Noah, since now he was saved from the death that overtook the whole world, and was delivered, both he and his children, to possess the whole earth himself. Indeed, he stepped from the earth to the altar; as Israel of old did sing on the shore of the red Sea: But, as they, he soon forgat; he rendered evil to God for good.[9]

There are some who have suggested that his drinking of the wine from his vineyard was an accident. Really? Why was Noah building a vineyard? Although the text does not say that Noah deliberately built a vineyard in order to make intoxicating wine, I think it is very likely that he did. Therefore, his drunkenness was not innocent.

Even in a fallen condition, Noah should have been respected by his sons. However, Ham's first action was to gossip about his father's nakedness. This was a disrespectful attitude. But it would not have been respectful to ignore their father's condition, either, which was why Shem and Japheth took action to cover Noah, and to do so without judgment, gossip, or condemnation. Shem and Japheth honored their father, but Ham did not.

For this reason, it seems somewhat unfair at first sight that Noah would curse not Ham but Canaan. However, the reason may be that Noah was speaking prophetically, knowing that the sin that Ham had begun would find greater conclusion in the actions of Canaan and his descendants. Calvin had this to say about why God chose to curse only one of Ham's sons, rather than all of them. He says:

---

9. John Bunyan (ed. Paul F. Taylor), *Genesis: A Commentary* (Leicester, UK: J6D Publications, Kindle Editions, 2009), Kindle Locations 5140–5143.

Another question is also proposed; namely, why among the many sons of Ham, God chooses one to be smitten? But let not our curiosity here indulge itself too freely; let us remember that the judgments of God are, not in vain, called "a great deep," and that it would be a degrading thing for God, before whose tribunal we all must one day stand, to be subjected to our judgments, or rather to our foolish temerity. He chooses whom he sees good, that he may show forth in them an example of his grace and kindness; others he appoints to a different end, that they may be proofs of his anger and severity. Here, although the minds of men are blinded, let every one of us, conscious of his own infirmity, learn rather to ascribe praise to God's justice, than plunge, with insane audacity, into the profound abyss. While God held the whole seed of Ham as obnoxious to the curse, he mentions the Canaanites by name, as those whom he would curse above all others. And hence we infer that this judgment proceeded from God, because it was proved by the event itself. What would certainly be the condition of the Canaanites, Noah could not know by human means. Wherefore in things obscure and hidden, the Spirit directed his tongue.[10]

God did not make a mistake in His treatment of either Ham or Canaan. God knew what He was doing and what the results of His actions would be.

---

10. Calvin, *Commentary on Genesis*, http://www.ccel.org/ccel/calvin/calcom01.xv.i.html.

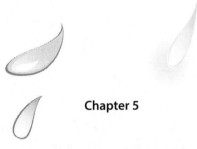

Chapter 5

The History of the Ancient World

Ancient civilizations seemed to be very clever, very quickly. How did so many of these civilizations develop such amazing technologies in such a short space of time? The world abounds with examples of such advanced civilizations, and secular historians find these a source of amazement. New discoveries cause secular historical paradigms to be constantly rewritten. When a new civilization seems too advanced for any suitable theory, it leads some people to develop weird and wacky ideas about ancient visits by space travelers or beings from other dimensions.

Instead of being led astray by such concepts, it behooves creationists to take a calm, sober look at the evidence, firmly convinced of our presupposition that God is in control and that His Word is true.

Recent history has been littered with examples of strange findings. At one time, the Bible was ridiculed because it spoke of a people group called the Hittites. No such people group was known until their cities were discovered in the 19th century.

Conventional "evolutionary"-type views about the development of societies so often seem to offer explanations that leave one dissatisfied. How were the Egyptians able to build their remarkable pyramids? Why did so many civilizations spring up in Mesopotamia so quickly? How did ancient people groups make constructions like Stonehenge or Carnac with such apparent scientific accuracy?

While individual answers to each of these conundrums need to be researched, the more pressing problem is to see all of these matters through biblical spectacles — through our presupposition that God created this world about 6,000 years ago and deluged it about 4,400 years ago.

When Did Civilization Begin?

If we really need to answer such a question, we can tell that we have been evolutionized. Even as creationists, we sometimes have to take stock and realize that evolutionary thinking has permeated our language in so many aspects.

In Genesis 2, we read about the first recorded occasion that God spoke to Adam.

> And the LORD God commanded the man, saying, "Of every tree of the garden you may freely eat; but of the tree of the knowledge of good and evil you shall not eat, for in the day that you eat of it you shall surely die" (Genesis 2:16–17).

The events of Genesis 2 took place on the sixth day of the creation week. God had only just made Adam, and He directed his attention toward the trees. This presupposes that Adam understood what a tree was. How would he know? God had created him with language. Language is not something that had to develop. From his very first day on earth, Adam was able to understand language. So was Eve, and together they were completely able to converse. Moreover, the passage above shows that Adam could understand abstract concepts. God expected Adam to understand that one tree was not to be eaten from. God also explained that when he ate of it, he would *surely* die. Notice that God did not say "if you eat" — God knew that Adam would eat of it. The phrase translated as *surely die* actually implies a process of death. God did not tell Adam that he would instantly drop dead, but that the process of death would start as soon as he ate from that tree. We also understand from this that Adam was capable of understanding things that he had not yet experienced. For God's sanction to mean anything, Adam had to have understood it, which means that he knew what the word "die" meant, even though he had not yet died nor seen anyone die.

Why am I belaboring this point? I am going through this matter to show that the basic cultural information necessary was already part of Adam's makeup at his creation. Adam was created civilized, with the abilities to enjoy the fruits of culture and civilization.

After the account of Cain killing Abel in Genesis 4, we get a brief discussion on what happens next. In Genesis 4:17 we read that Cain built a city and named it after one of his sons, Enoch. Note that this is not the same Enoch as the one in the promised lineage, but the name means the same thing — *teacher*. Cain therefore had the ability to build a city and Enoch was a teacher. Where did these abilities come from? Again, we must emphasize that we do not believe they evolved. Sometimes even creationists are looking through Scripture for reasons for certain phenomena developing. No reasons are necessary. These aspects of culture and civilization were part of the way that God had created people.

Not only were cultural aspects "built in" to humanity, but, very early on, people found ways of adapting these cultural practices — sometimes not just adapting them, but perverting them. Lamech, for example, was fully conversant with the existing cultural norm that there should be one man for one woman in marriage. However, he decided that he could alter this by taking a second wife and by arbitrarily creating his own laws that went beyond the sanctions given by God. We have discussed this matter of Lamech's sins in the chapter "The World before the Flood."

Perhaps the cultural advances of Lamech's sons were somewhat nobler. Lamech had three sons. Jabal dwelt in tents and kept livestock. This sounds rather different from Abel's pattern of keeping sheep, which we assume were for sacrifice and priestly duties. It is likely then that Jabal was going outside God's statement that humans and animals should eat vegetables, and was perhaps beginning to eat meat.

There does not seem to be anything wrong with Jubal's occupation, on the other hand. Jubal played musical instruments, both stringed (harp) and wind (flute). It is likely that he made these himself, so concepts of tonality, pitch, and timbre were now available.

Tubal-Cain was a craftsman. This, in itself, requires culture. The materials with which he worked required science and technology. He worked with bronze or brass. The Hebrew word that is translated as bronze or brass implies simple metals that are easy to extract from their ores. This could probably be metals like copper and tin. The word also implies alloying, so it is likely that Tubal-Cain had experimented with mixing metals. Today's bronze, for example, is an alloy of copper and tin. Higher technology, however, is required for iron. Iron is rather difficult to extract from its ore. To do so requires a reducing agent, such as charcoal, and superheated temperatures such as those produced in blast furnaces. It is noteworthy that historians often speak about technological ages, such as stone age, bronze age, and iron age. Yet Tubal-Cain was able to span both a personal bronze age and a personal iron age. It is likely that the assignment of certain civilizations to "ages" is arbitrary, and may speak simply of what materials were available, rather than what their cultural abilities were. An example of this would be the extraordinary regional "market" in flint tools that seems to have existed throughout the British Isles in the times that the megaliths, such as Stonehenge, were built. I will suggest later that such structures were developed by peoples who were migrating following the Tower of Babel incident. The fact that they used flint suggests only that they had not had time to become established and therefore used readily available materials, whereas the market suggests a high degree of civilization and culture.

Post-Flood Memories

The previous section suggested that the level of sophistication before the Flood was great. It makes sense to suppose, therefore, that Noah and his sons were able to pass on much of this knowledge and skill base to their immediate descendants. Therefore, the Table of Nations in Genesis 10 refers to people groups who inherited considerable levels of civilization. Once they were able to settle, therefore, they would be able to exploit these cultural abilities. This may have some relevance to God's command after the Flood to fill the earth and subdue it, knowing that if the people settled too long, the development of civilizing factors would hinder the earth's recolonization. This is, of course, what actually happened with the Tower of Babel incident.

If we look at the various tables of descent in Genesis 10, we can make a few tentative assumptions. For example, we read that it was in the days of Peleg that the earth was divided (10:25). It is unlikely that this refers to physical break-up of the continents, which is much more likely to have occurred in the early days of the Flood. Therefore, the division of the world in Peleg's time most likely refers to the division of people groups as they were scattered across the world following the Tower of Babel incident in Genesis 11.

Peleg was likely to have been born while Nimrod was at the height of his powers. Or some suggest he rose in power after the linguistic division.

> Cush begot Nimrod; he began to be a mighty one on the earth. He was a mighty hunter before the LORD; therefore it is said, "Like Nimrod the mighty hunter before the LORD." And the beginning of his kingdom was Babel, Erech, Accad, and Calneh, in the land

of Shinar. From that land he went to Assyria and built Nineveh, Rehoboth Ir, Calah, and Resen between Nineveh and Calah (that *is* the principal city) (Genesis 10:8–12).

Nimrod did not start mighty. He became mighty. He was a mighty hunter. What does this mean? It is unlikely to refer to modern hunting, but seems to suggest hunting people. Therefore, this is not a noble calling. He was a mighty hunter before the Lord. The Hebrew word for before is *panîm*, which actually means "in the face of. . . ." Therefore, Nimrod was someone who hunted people, and did so shaking his fist at God. This suggests that he was a military tyrant. These verses tell us that Babel was one of the cities that he built, so it could have been the focus of his empire. When we are told that "he went to Assyria," this sounds rather like a military invasion. Nimrod could probably have been leading a military government that was conquering areas colonized by other people, with a view to preventing scattering over the planet. This, of course, fits entirely with the account of the rebellion at Babel in Genesis 11.

Genesis 10, therefore, suggests a rapid development of culture and civilization, at least some of which was of a negative quality. It would make sense to suppose that the various early civilizations, which we know about, grew up in the early generations after the Flood. This would also explain why so many early civilizations sprang up, "suddenly," in the Near East.

One of the difficulties with such a view is that contemporary secular dating often suggests that artifacts and constructions are older than our possible date for a worldwide Flood.

Dates and Dynasties in Egypt

The Flood occurred about 2,350 years before Christ. Yet the Pyramid of Giza is dated to about 2560 B.C. Something does not compute properly. Either the Bible is wrong or the secular dates are wrong.

Of course, secularists immediately assume that the Bible is wrong, because this is always their presupposition. Our presupposition, however, is that the Bible is true. Therefore, there must be something wrong with Egyptian dates.

So many Egyptian dates are set relative to the dating of pharaohs and dynasties. Recent research has suggested that dynasties may have overlapped somewhat in Egyptian history.[1]

---

1. John Ashton and David Down, *Unwrapping the Pharaohs* (Green Forest, AR: Master Books, 2006).

Traditionally, it has always been assumed that the pharaoh at the time of Moses and the Exodus was Rameses II, and his dates have been given as about 1304–1237 B.C. Because no archaeological evidence of Semitic slaves has been found in the 14th century B.C, it has often been assumed that this proves the Bible to be wrong. However, the new chronology places Rameses II in the mid 10th century B.C. This would makes Rameses contemporaneous with Solomon's son, Rehoboam. Ashton and Down suggest that this might identify him as Shishak (1 Kings 14:25).[2]

This new chronology gives us a different candidate for the Exodus pharaoh — Khasekemre-Neferhotep I. The circumstances surrounding Neferhotep are chaotic. There were two pharaohs immediately before Neferhotep. Amenemhet III was probably the pharaoh at the time of the slaughter of the Israelite babies. His daughter, Sobekneferu, succeeded him for just four years. She was probably the one who brought up Moses. She had no successor, so her dynasty — the 12th — came to an end. Thus, Neferhotep was the founder of the 13th dynasty. But his mummy has never been found. He just seems to have disappeared, at a time when a mysterious people group called the Hyksos were able to just take over Egypt without a battle. Neferhotep was succeeded by his brother, not his son, Wahneferhotep, who also seems to have disappeared!

Ashton and Down suggest that the explanations for these facts are as follows. Neferhotep has no mummy, because he drowned at the bottom of the Red Sea after the Israelites had crossed. Wahneferhotep did not succeed because he was already dead, in the 10th plague. The Hyksos were able to temporarily take over Egypt because the Egyptian army was also drowned at the bottom of the Red Sea.

If this new chronology actually works, as it seems to, this would place Joseph in Egypt at the time of Pharaoh Sesostris I. He seems to have been a good, caring king, and this would fit with his reliance on Joseph's counsel. Sesostris's dates used to be suggested as 1971–1928 B.C., but the revised chronology places him as ruler in 1681 B.C., which is when Joseph would have been sold into slavery. Sesostris appears, later in life, to have had a very powerful vizier named Mentuhotep. Ashton and Down suggest that Mentuhotep and Joseph are the same person.[3] Further corroboration of this conjecture is found in the text on a column of Sesostris's era, which reads:

---

2. Ibid., p. 175.
3. Ibid., p. 79–87.

I was in mourning on my throne. Those of the palace were in grief, my heart was in great affliction. Because Hapy [the river god] had failed to come in time in a period of seven years. Grain was scant, kernels were dried up, scarce was every kind of food. Every man robbed his twin, those who entered did not go. Children cried, youngsters fell, the hearts of the old were grieving; legs drawn up, they hugged the ground, their arms clasped about them. Courtiers were needy, temples were shut, shrines covered with dust, everyone was in distress.[4]

This sounds rather like an account of the seven years of famine, predicted by Joseph's interpretation of Pharaoh's dream.

A lot more such information can be gleaned, by studying Ashton and Down's book *Unwrapping the Pharaohs*. The point in giving this information here is to show that it is not necessary to accept conventional and traditional dates for early civilizations. Skeptical historians have a vested interest in undermining biblical accounts. We have seen that a revised chronology for Egyptian pharaohs is at least possible, and that such research is consistent with our presupposition that the Bible is true.

Flood Legends

Given our renewed determination to assume that early civilizations were actually post-Flood developments, as outlined in Genesis 10, one corollary of such an idea is to assume that many worldwide people groups might share historical accounts that bear some relationship to the history as recorded in the Bible. An obvious place to start is to see whether or not other people groups have myths about a Flood. It turns out that they do.

Charles Martin has documented a number of such Flood legends, focusing on three in detail. He has analyzed the biblical account of the Flood, alongside an account in the Hindu Mahābhārata and an account from the Kariña peoples.[5] It is fascinating to note the many similarities in these tales. All except the biblical account contain details that seem unlikely. This is what we would expect if the biblical account were the original and correct account, while all the others contain embellishments of varying degrees. Martin also briefly mentions accounts from the Epic of Gilgamesh, British Columbia, the Valmans of New Guinea, and the Hareskins of North America, to name but four. Tim Lovett includes a table of flood legends

---

4. Ibid., p. 84.
5. Charles Martin, *Flood Legends* (Green Forest, AR: Master Books, 2009), p. 121–130.

in his book *Noah's Ark: Thinking Outside the Box*.[6] In 2011, Eric Hovind and I had the privilege of interviewing Jeremy Wiles for our TV show, *Creation Today*.[7] Jeremy has spent a lifetime researching Flood legends from around the world. One video clip that we included showed Jeremy meeting an elderly Chinese gentleman who sang him an epic song about the Flood and the ark!

Research shows that there are many, many more accounts of the Flood around the world than just these. Again, the existence of these legends is what we would expect if the biblical account were true — which it is!

Babel Diaspora

The result of the arrogant and sinful actions of the citizens of Babel was that differences in languages were created by God. Today, we recognize that there are distinct language groups that bear no relationship to each other — a fact that is problematic for those with an evolutionary view of language development. This confusion of languages forced the people of the world to do what they should have done voluntarily — scatter over the face of the earth.

As they moved, they took their ideas with them. The principle error of the Babel people was to attempt to get to the heavens without God. The tower unto the heavens was probably a means of worshiping the stars and constellations, as if they were gods. This pagan practice is exactly what is suggested by Paul in Romans 1, as a natural consequence of failing to obey the true God.

As these people groups scattered, they would carry with them allusions to the pagan worship at Babel. Thus, structures like Stonehenge in Wiltshire, England, and Carnac, in Brittany, France, are aligned in remarkable ways to various astronomical events, such as the Solstice sunrise. The attempted worship of the created, rather than the Creator, is a common theme of such structures built by the early Babel diaspora. Such structures include Zimbabwe (in the country that was named after these remarkable stone buildings), Mayan temples, and Mesopotamian ziggurats. The people groups that created these religious yet scientific structures also have legends about the Flood.

---

6. Tim Lovett, *Noah's Ark: Thinking Outside the Box* (Green Forest, AR: Master Books, 2009).
7. Creation Today, http://www.creationtoday.org.

Summary

Evidences from post-Flood civilizations do not prove the authenticity of the Bible. That authenticity should never be in question. Rather, these evidences are consistent with our presupposition that the Bible is true. Early civilizations cannot be older than the Flood, and must be either recorded in Genesis 10, or descended from groups mentioned therein. Many of these civilizations have legends about a Flood. Readers are not to be alarmed when secular science produces dates or other "evidences" that suggest the Bible is wrong. The Bible is not wrong, and so-called researchers will catch up with what the Bible teaches eventually. Meanwhile, churches and pastors should not be afraid to teach this "early" history, because to do so is to take God at His word, and to give Him alone the glory.

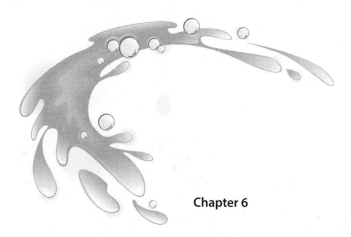

Chapter 6

Why Our Society Stopped Believing in the Flood

The prettiest capital city in Britain is not London; it is Edinburgh. If you visit the city you will want to see the castle where the crown jewels of the kings of Scotland are kept, and the Royal Mile leading to Holyrood Palace, where the queen stays when she is in the Scottish capital. If you want to see these and lots of other tourist sites, it is worth getting on one of the city's open-top tour buses. I took advantage of one of these informative experiences when I went on one of my numerous visits to Edinburgh. As the bus passed the Scottish Parliament building, we got to a spot where there is an excellent view of the rocky outcrops known as Salisbury Craggs. At this point, the tour guide said, "It was in the 18th century that the geologist James Hutton looked at these rocks and proved the Bible to be wrong."

Of course, I do not accept that the Bible is wrong. But who was James Hutton, and why should a tour operator assume that this man had proved the Bible to be wrong; and what did Salisbury Craggs have to do with it?

The Birth of Geological Science

There are many good histories around about the early days of geology and how geologists came to reject the Bible's time scale.[1] Geology is not a very old science, really — only about 200 years old or so.

---

1. In my opinion, the best historian of this fascinating period is Dr. Terry Mortenson of Answers in Genesis. I strongly recommend Terry's book *The Great Turning Point: The Church's Catastrophic Mistake on Geology — Before Darwin* (Green Forest, AR: Master Books, 2004).

It has often been said that the founder of modern geology was Nicolaus Steno (1638–1686). Steno, who was Dutch (original Dutch name Niels Steenson), published an important book in 1671 entitled *The Prodromus to a Dissertation Concerning Solids Naturally Contained within Solids* (a prodomus is a preliminary treatise). His great insight in this book was to introduce the concept of stratigraphy — the idea that, in a given rock system, the higher strata or layers were laid down after the lower layers, and so the higher layers are younger than the lower ones. Modern secular geologists love this idea, because they immediately suppose that these relative ages imply millions of years, so it comes as a shock to many such geologists to finds that Steno not only believed the Bible, but accepted a biblical time scale of about 6,000 years.[2] Steno's book came less than 20 years after James Ussher's *Annals of the World*, in which Ussher published his creation date of 4004 B.C. The famous scientist Isaac Newton was also working on a historical date for creation, of a similar order to that of Ussher, though his findings were eventually published posthumously in 1728.

Steno viewed his geological research through, as it were, biblical spectacles. For example, in his study of the geology of Tuscany, he says this:

> In regard to the first aspect of the earth Scripture and Nature agree in this, that all things were covered with water; how and when this aspect began, and how long it lasted, Nature says not, Scripture relates.[3]

Steno notes that where "nature" does not give him an empirical date, the Bible is very clear on the dating. Therefore, the concept of relative ages of the rock strata is not unbiblical, and, indeed, is logical. It is the millions of years suggested for such events that are problematic. Steno was not alone in his analysis; a number of other writers of the period published similar views, such as John Woodward and Johann Lehmann.

James Hutton

Abraham Werner had suggested a system whereby rocks were divided into four groups, called Primary, Secondary, Tertiary, and Quaternary. He

---

2. Tas Walker, "Geological Pioneer Nicolas Steno Was a Biblical Creationist," *Journal of Creation* 22(1) (2008): p. 93–98.
3. J.G. Winter (translator), Nicholaus Steno (1631–1686), *The Prodromus of Nicholaus Steno's Dissertation Concerning a Solid Body Enclosed by Process of Nature Within a Solid*, an English version with an introduction and explanatory notes (New York: Hafner Publishing Company, Inc., 1968), p. 263–269, quoted in reference 2.

supposed that these rocks precipitated at different stages of a long global flood. However, he rejected the biblical time scale, and supposed that this flood had lasted a million years. Some geologists classified the rocks as creation rocks (primary), flood rocks (secondary), post-flood rocks (tertiary) and more recent rocks (quaternary).

James Hutton (1726–1797) was an Edinburgh physician. In his spare time he studied rocks. In particular, he was intrigued by both Salisbury Cragg and Siccar Point, the latter being a geological feature a few miles east of Edinburgh. Both features present lower strata of near vertical bedding planes covered by near horizontal strata. Hutton proposed that the lower rocks had originally been laid horizontal and then moved by some seismic activity. There is nothing in that view for creationists to differ with. He then looked at the unconformity between the two strata and proposed that the lower strata must have been eroded over millions of years, before the upper layer was deposited. Hutton proposed that he could see no beginning to the rock record that he observed, and therefore suggested that the earth was infinitely old. It should be pointed out, in passing, that a better explanation for Siccar Point, from a creationist viewpoint, is discussed in our chapter "During the Flood."

The next generation of geologists seemed as if they were moving back to a biblical position. Georges Cuvier (1768–1832) proposed a theory known as *catastrophism*. Unfortunately, he did not believe in just one flood, but interpreted the rock structures by means of a lot of catastrophic events. He believed that Noah's Flood was the only one of these that happened after humans were created, and his viewpoint, which gained a considerable following, required millions of years. Like Werner, he had compromised on the truth of Scripture — that very same truth that Steno had used to interpret everything that he saw.

Uniformitarianism

Although Hutton's model had no beginning (he believed the earth to be infinitely old), he was nevertheless the father of uniformitarianism — the idea that past geological processes must have happened at the same rate as today. His ideas were taken up by the Scottish lawyer Charles Lyell in his three-volume work *Principles of Geology*. It is noteworthy that the first volume was published in 1830, while Charles Darwin's legendary voyage on HMS *Beagle* began in 1831. Darwin took a copy of Lyell's first volume with him, and had the second volume (published 1832) shipped out to him. It can safely be said, then, that Darwin was thoroughly immersed in Lyell's old-earth ideas by the time he began to produce his evolutionary ideas.[4]

Lyell believed that all past geological processes had proceeded at the same rate as current geological processes. His famous concept, which may be apocryphal, was that "the present is the key to the past." It is this concept that is opposed by 2 Peter 3. What is less well known is Lyell's motivation for his ideas. In a letter to his sister, he said this:

> I had conceived the idea, about five or six years ago, that if ever the Mosaic chronology could be set down without giving offense, it would be in an historical sketch.[5]

When this Victorian language is properly understood, its impact is devastating. Lyell wanted to "set down," or overturn, Mosaic chronology. It was his deliberate purpose, therefore, to undermine the time scales that we read about in the Bible. He hoped to do this "without offense" — in other words, with the acquiescence of Christian leaders, and his methodology for so doing would be to rewrite the history of the earth. That Lyell was phenomenally successful in his aims is made apparent by the state of the Church today, and also in the ready acceptance of unbiblical Darwinian ideas of evolution. Even in his own lifetime, too many Christian leaders lacked the ability to discern between actual scientific observation and old-age conjecture. For this reason, errors began to creep into the churches that expounded a compromised old-earth position. These errors included Thomas Chalmer's *gap theory* and George Stanley Faber's *day-age theory*. This era of compromise in the Christian church is brilliantly fictionalized in Nick Daniels' novel *The Gentlemen's Conspiracy*.[6]

Consequences of Compromise

Why is the above discussion relevant in a book about the Flood? It is relevant, because a natural corollary of compromise on the age of the earth is to accept a local flood theory, or to reject the concept of a biblical flood altogether. Steno had early realized that the fossils in the rocks were likely to have been formed during the Flood. For the geologist who takes the Bible seriously, the overwhelming majority of fossils must have been formed

---

4. For more discussion on the relationship between Lyell and Darwin, please see my biography of Darwin: Ian McNaughton and Paul F. Taylor, *Darwin and Darwinism: 150 Years Later* (Leominster, UK: Day One Publications, 2009).

5. K.M. Lyell, *Life, Letters, and Journals of Sir Charles Lyell* (London: John Murray, 1881), Vol. 1, p. 253.

6. Nick Daniels, *The Gentlemen's Conspiracy* (Portland, OR: Risen Books, 2009).

during the Flood. However, if we allow for millions of years, we are allowing that the majority of fossils were formed in those millions of years before mankind. Therefore, there could not have been a violent, worldwide flood, because there is no evidence for it, once we have arbitrarily decided that the actual evidence for the Flood came from millions of years earlier.

A second problem with these old-earth compromises is that they undermine the foundations of the gospel. In Genesis 1, we read that God made a perfect world. How could such a world really be perfect if the rocks beneath Adam and Eve's feet contained the fossilized evidence of death, disease, and suffering? And if death was already in the world, for what purpose did Jesus have to go to the Cross, considering that His work was to destroy the death that had supposedly entered the world through Adam?

The Scriptural Geologists

One of the great values of Dr. Terry Mortenson's work, referenced earlier, is in bringing to our attention the fact that not all early geologists compromised on the truth of Scripture. An unorganized but industrious group of Bible-believing geologists — often referred to as the Scriptural Geologists — were busy doing their research and battling against old-earth compromises. Mortenson has written about these interesting people, both academically[7] and at an easy-to-read level, in his book *The Great Turning Point*. The reader will find it interesting to look up Mortenson's articles on these men. For now, I will present some information about two of these geologists.

It is worth starting with George Bugg, because he wrote a massive two-volume work with the title *Scriptural Geology*. In this book, Bugg detailed his philosophy on how to marry science and the Bible.

> I allow, as I before allowed, that sacred writers may be silent about science or even ignorant of it, without impeaching their infallibility as recorders of divine revelation. But whatever they do declare, and on whatever subject (as we before observed from Bishop Horsley) is certainly true. They were under divine and supernatural guidance, and therefore personal *ignorance* in the *writer* is no *defect*; and *error is impossible*.[8] (italics from original)

---

7. See the series of peer-reviewed articles, beginning with Terry Mortenson, "British Scriptural Geologists in the First Half of the Nineteenth Century: Part 1," *Journal of Creation*, 11(2):221–252 (August 1997).

8. George Bugg, *Scriptural Theology*, quoted in Terry Mortenson, *The Great Turning Point: The Church's Catastrophic Mistake on Geology — Before Darwin* (Green Forest, AR: Master Books, 2004), http://www.answersingenesis.org/articles/gtp/george-bugg.

Bugg is stating that it is completely acceptable for a scientist to study his subject, but that where the Bible touches on that subject, it speaks without error. This is exactly the principle that should be adopted by evangelical scientists today.

Bugg was born in 1769 in Leicestershire. He used the conversion experience of his late teens to argue against Anglo-Catholic doctrines of baptismal regeneration. As an ordained Anglican minister, it appears that he enjoyed good relations with, and the respect of, non-conformist ministers as well as fellow Anglican evangelicals. *Scriptural Geology* was published in 1836, by which time Lyell's uniformitarian work had already been published. Mortenson reports that Bugg was concerned about how old-earth views misrepresented the nature of God.

> He objected that the old-earth geological *theory* about the *time and processes of the formation* of that structure was inconsistent with the nature of God. He asked, where is the wisdom, kindness, and justice of many revolutions on the earth before man sinned, which destroyed myriads of creatures? The Bible, on the other hand, taught that God had originally made a perfect, mature, productive, and fertile creation and that there was a holy and wise reason for the one destructive catastrophe, the Flood.[9] (italics from original)

Bugg saw the Flood as the principle explanation for the fossil record, as do creationists today.

> Likewise, Bugg believed that the nature of the Flood explained the fossil record, whereas Cuvier's theory did not. For example, the Flood would be expected to have buried plants at all levels and to mix together land and marine animals and he cited evidence that this was the case. He also quoted evidence from Jameson's appended notes to Cuvier's *Theory of the Earth* and Buckland's report of a recent discovery (in 1826) of an opossum found in the lower Oolite, well below the level it should have appeared according to Cuvier's theory. Added to this was evidence from Conybeare, Phillips, and Jameson showing that supposedly extinct shellfish and land animals were mixed in recent deposits with the remains of existing species, in contradiction to Cuvier's theory, but just exactly as the Flood would be expected to produce.[10]

9. Ibid.
10. Ibid.

Why was a man like Bugg, with little formal scientific training, so keen to take on the emerging heavyweights of both the uniformitarian and catastrophist old-earth geologists? Mortenson again:

> Bugg clearly stated that he engaged in this debate because of his love for the truth. He perceived there was a battle going on. But it was not science against religion. He had no antipathy to the pursuit of knowledge about the physical creation by the method of experimentation and observation. Rather, he saw it as a battle between the Christian faith and ancient heathen, atheistic ideas, which were being revived primarily by continental philosophers and were penetrating the Church. This battle was really only a part of a long-standing strategy of Satan to undermine faith in the inspiration and infallible truth of Scripture, a battle especially intense in the minds of the young men training for ministry at British universities.[11]

George Young (1777–1848) was more accomplished in geology. Like Bugg, he became a clergyman, ministering in the ancient Yorkshire fishing village of Whitby. Unlike Bugg, he had studied some geology at university, under the tutorage of John Playfair — the most prominent advocate of James Hutton's views. Young also published a book called *Scriptural Geology* (1838), as well as his earlier study, *A Geological Survey of the Yorkshire Coast,* in 1828. Mortenson quotes Young's views on geology:

> The researches of the geologist are far from being unworthy of the Christian, or the philosopher: for, while they enlarge the bounds of our knowledge, and present a wide field for intellectual employment and innocent pleasure, they may serve to conduct us to the glorious Being.[12]

That he should have felt the need to write thus shows that Young was aware of the fact that geology was being seen as something that undermined the Christian faith. Nevertheless, Young's geological writing was regarded highly even by old-earth compromisers like Adam Sedgwick, who commented on the "excellent details" of Young's Yorkshire Survey.

Young's work sometimes reads remarkably like that of modern creationists. For example, read his rebuttal of old-earth fossilization theories, again quoted by Mortenson.

---

11. Ibid.
12. Ibid.

But the primary focus of Young's rebuttal [of old-earth fossiliza-tion models] was on the idea that the fossils buried in the strata were situated in the place where the plants and animals had lived, died, and were later buried. He instead argued that the evidence pointed to the conclusion that these creatures had been transported by flood waters and deposited with the sediments of the strata.

He rejected the *in situ* theory for plants because, first, no exist-ing peat bog was thick enough to produce the vast coal seams, which were also interspersed with ocean-deposited sediments. He cited evidence and arguments from Lyell and Phillips to support his contention that upright fossil trees and stems, so often associated with the coal, had been transported to their positions before being buried.[13]

Through his work, Young maintained a clear biblical witness and opposed ideas that he saw as undermining the authority of Scripture. Modern cre-ationists would do well to follow his example, in his knowledge of Scripture, his thoroughness in opposing unscriptural ideas, and also in the respectful and non-confrontational manner in which he treated his opponents.

Conclusion

The writer of Ecclesiastes says:

That which has been is what will be, that which is done is what will be done, and there is nothing new under the sun (Ecclesiastes 1:9).

The history of the early days of geology is like an account of the current debate over creation and evolution. It is a history that shows a desire among some to deliberately undermine the authority of Scripture, and to do so in the name of science. It is a history that shows the rush among too many Christian leaders to compromise on the truth of Genesis. And it is a history that shows there are always godly men who will fight for the truth and for the honor of God's name.

---

13. Ibid.

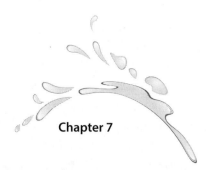

Chapter 7

The Flood and the Modern Creationist Movement

Does the modern creationist movement have a recognized date of birth? If it did, then its year of birth would probably be 1961, because this was the year that Drs. John Whitcomb and Henry Morris published their seminal work *The Genesis Flood*. I had read a couple of worthy but light-weight books before I bought my first copy in 1979. At the time, I wondered about whether or not, as an 18-year-old book, it was a bit out of date. I never imagined that I would witness seeing the book still in print on its 50th anniversary.

My Connection with *The Genesis Flood*

I was born in 1961, so I am the same age as the book. I was saved in early 1977, and was about to begin studying for A-levels in math, physics, and chemistry at school.[1] In early 1978, I was able to earn some of my own money by taking on a part-time job at a local Christian bookshop. It was at this shop that I first came across creationist literature, because the shop manager was very keen to promote the truth of Genesis. By far the most respectable of these books was a difficult-to-read scientific study called *The*

---

1. A-levels were (and still are) the principle university entrance qualification taken by 18-year-olds in England, Wales, and Northern Ireland. Math (or, as the British would have it, maths), physics, and chemistry were the usual three subjects to take if one intended further study in the physical sciences.

Genesis Flood. In spite of its difficulty, I knew that I needed to purchase a copy, to attempt to understand my belief in the literal truth of Genesis at a higher intellectual level.

Fast forward over 40 years. In 2005, I was invited to work for Answers in Genesis (UK/Europe). Two months before my posting was to begin, I was invited to fly out with the other AiG-UK speakers to Lynchburg, Virginia, to attend the Answers in Genesis Mega Conference. One of the speakers was Dr. John Whitcomb, one of the authors of *The Genesis Flood.* He reported that Dr. Morris was ill (Henry Morris died shortly after this), but he gave a lively and important history of the impact of their book. After the talk, I decided to join the queue to get an autographed copy of the book, even though I already had a copy at home. The idea of getting the signature of one of my heroes of the faith was very important. As I handed the book to Dr. Whitcomb to sign, he glanced at my delegate badge.

"Paul Taylor!" he exclaimed. "You are the gentleman who has just started working with Answers in Genesis UK!"

The fact that one of my heroes of the faith had actually heard about me made me feel ten feet tall, I can tell you!

In his address to the conference, Dr. Whitcomb listed two major negative responses to *The Genesis Flood,* which were leading Christians away from the truth of the Book of Genesis and, in particular, undermining Christians' belief in a worldwide global Flood.[2]

Negative Responses to *The Genesis Flood*

Dr. Whitcomb first analyzed progressive creationism, which is the label for the views of astronomer Hugh Ross and his ministry, Reasons to Believe. Dr. Whitcomb describes Ross's views thus:

> He believes that creation began many billions of years ago with a so-called "big bang"; that animals were supernaturally and periodically created (not evolved) through millions of years; that Adam's rebellion against God did not cause death in the animal kingdom; and that the Flood was local in extent. He believes that the Bible's 66 books are fully inspired, but need to be reinterpreted in the light of a 67th book, namely modern science.[3]

---

2. John Whitcomb, "The History and Impact of *The Genesis Flood,*" Institute for Creation Research, 2006, http://www.icr.org/article/history-impact-book-the-genesis-flood/.
3. Ibid.

Dr. Whitcomb emphasized that a belief in millions of years is not a minor aberration. He pointed out that Progressive Creationism requires believing that the majority of fossils were formed before the creation of mankind and, therefore, do not need explaining by means of the worldwide Flood of Genesis 6–8. Therefore, it is not only Genesis chapter 1 that gets rewritten — Genesis 6–8 have to be interpreted figuratively, as soon as we move away from a belief in a literal six days.

Dr. Whitcomb then focused a large portion of his talk on the subject of the Intelligent Design Movement. Many creationists are eager to exploit the arguments of the ID movement. Whitcomb cautioned creationists from wholehearted support for ID. He noted that Philip E. Johnson, one of the most prominent ID advocates, had argued that the Bible was not to be used in opposing evolution.

> Get the Bible and the book of Genesis out of the debate, because you do not want to raise the so-called Bible-science dichotomy. Phrase the argument in such a way that you can get it heard in the secular academy and in a way that tends to unify the religious dissenters. That means concentrating on, "Do you need a Creator to do the creating, or can nature do it on its own?" and refusing to get sidetracked onto other issues. . . . They'll ask, "What do you think of Noah's flood?" or something like that. Never bite on such questions because they'll lead you into a trackless wasteland and you'll never get out of it.[4]

The reason why such an approach is wrong is that Jesus is the Creator, so to refuse to speak about Him is a major omission. Whitcomb put it thus:

> In response, we humbly insist that *it is essential to believe the Genesis record of origins in order to please God.*[5]

The danger is for people to see the creationist issue as only involving opposition to evolution. This is not the case. The Apostle Peter, in a passage that we creationists quote frequently, says this:

> [Know] this first: that scoffers will come in the last days, walking according to their own lusts, and saying, "Where is the promise of His coming? For since the fathers fell asleep, all things continue as they were from the beginning of creation." For this

---

4. "Berkeley's Radical," in *Touchstone* 15:5 (June, 2002): p. 41.
5. Ibid., emphasis original.

they willfully forget: that by the word of God the heavens were of old, and the earth standing out of water and in the water, by which the world that then existed perished, being flooded with water (2 Peter 3:3–6).

The scoffers forget two things. These two things are not forgotten by chance. The forgetfulness is willful. The two things that they willfully forget are (1) God created and (2) God sent a Flood. It is not enough for us to oppose evolution. If we fail to honor Christ as Creator, we dishonor God. But it is not even enough to proclaim the truth that God created. We have to proclaim that God created in the manner in which He said He created, and with the time scale with which He said He created. And we must also acknowledge that there was a worldwide Flood. Belief in the truth of the account of the Flood is not an optional extra to tag on to our creationism. Such belief is central to our creationism.

Only the Credulous Believe

The reaction of skeptics to the concept of a worldwide Flood has often put creationists on the defensive. This is especially true if the creationists only view matters in terms of opposing evolution and not in terms of the proclamation of the gospel. If creationists concentrate on simple anti-evolutionism, then they tend to be embarrassed by the Flood, not wanting to add the difficulty of defending the Flood to the difficulty of defending biblical creation. Let me say, before I analyze the criticism of skeptics, that I do not think that creationists should have this embarrassment. Rather, they should embrace and rejoice in their defense of the Flood. Genesis 6–8 explains so much of the world around us, and it explains the science of the past. The history of the Flood is an essential partner of the history of creation.

Writing in *The Skeptical Review*, the atheist Farrell Till singled out belief in a worldwide Flood for withering criticism.

> If Bible fundamentalists are honest, then, they will have to admit that the Genesis writer intended his story to be understood as an account of a flood that had covered the entire earth. In other words, he expected us to believe that within the space of forty days enough water rained down or rose from "the fountains of the deep" to cover the highest mountain on earth to a depth of 15 cubits (7:20). In prescientific times when people knew very little about geography

and meteorology, a claim like this could find general acceptance, but in modern times only the very credulous can believe it.[6]

The reason for Till's incredulity is that he analyzes the Genesis account, using current presuppositions, exactly as Peter warned in the Scripture quoted above. For example, Till simply adds 15 cubits to the height of Everest and calculates the volume of water required to make such a covering. He then calculates the rate at which rain would have to fall, and reckons that the rainfall quantity would be too great. In so doing, he makes erroneous assumptions. He assumes that the topography of the pre-Flood world would be the same as the post-Flood world and also that the one source of floodwater would be the rain. Neither of these assumptions is sensible. As far as I know, no creationist makes such assumptions. So, for all his math calculations, Till is actually tilting at windmills. At the end of his article, Till makes what he thinks is a highly sarcastic put-down of the concept of divine omnipotence. The old saying goes — many a true word is spoken in jest!

> Yes, if we concede the existence of an omniscient, omnipotent deity who personally engineered every phase of the flood, then presumably that would make anything possible. . . . If one wants to believe that, then the story makes perfectly good sense. If, however, anyone puts any premium at all on common sense, he will have to consider the story a myth from prescientific times.[7]

Of course, we do not really expect atheists and skeptics to believe in a worldwide Flood, because they do not believe in God and they do not accept the Bible as a credible source of evidence. It is depressing, however, when we find the same attitude exhibited by supposed evangelical Christians. For example, Dr. Denis Alexander claims to be an evangelical Christian. He is the director of the Faraday Institute — a society for Christians who are practicing scientists. His acceptance of evolution would, in my view, cause problems for the famous scientist after whom his institute is named.[8]

---

6. Farrell Till, "Common Sense and Noah's Flood," *The Skeptical Review* (March/April 1993), http://theskepticalreview.com/tsrmag/2noah93.html.

7. Ibid.

8. Dr. Andy McIntosh, Professor of Thermodynamics at the University of Leeds, gave a powerful lecture entitled *Michael Faraday: Man of Science and Man of God* at Westminster Chapel, London, in April 2010. In this lecture, he devastatingly demonstrated the incompatibility of theistic evolution with the personal theology and scientific work of Faraday. This lecture is available on DVD, in UK Region 2 PAL format, from Answers in Genesis (UK), http://www.answersingenesis.org.uk.

Alexander lists a number of models for interpreting Genesis in his book *Creation or Evolution: Do We Have to Choose?* In describing his favored model, which is Model C in his nomenclature, he says this:

> The flood is a further issue that requires addressing in connection with the proposed *homo divinus*[9] of model C. There is no reason not to accept the Genesis account of the flood as a historical event in which the godly Noah and his family were saved. But model C would interpret the flood account as referring to the saving of those who "walked with God" (Genesis 6:9), together with the livestock that were essential for their welfare, through a local, albeit devastating, flood that affected the area of the Euphrates valley and its surrounds. *In fact there is no geological evidence for a global flood*, and the language of Genesis that refers to "every living thing on the face of the earth" being "wiped out," may very well refer to that "world" with which Noah and his family were familiar.[10]

The emphasized clause shows the extent of Alexander's unbiblical presupposition. If he started with the presupposition that the Bible was true, he would observe that the earth is literally covered with evidence of the Flood, by virtue of every sedimentary rock and fossil-bearing strata he can trip over. But because he is prepared to believe in death before the Fall, in contradiction to the clear words of the New Testament as well as the Old, he automatically assigns the fossils to millions of years before Adam, and fails to acknowledge the clear geological evidence for the Flood. In short, the actual evidence does not fit his worldview. Despite claiming to be a Christian — and an evangelical Christian at that — his science is, to all intents and purposes, atheistic.

What about Mount St. Helens?

You could never recreate this photograph today. It was taken on May 17, 1980.

---

9. *Homo divinus*, a term used by Alexander, was originally invented by the late Dr. John Stott, to describe how he believed God turned the first evolved ape-man into a real human being by breathing into him.
10. Denis R. Alexander, *Creation or Evolution: Do We Have to Choose?* (Oxford, UK: Monarch Books, 2008), p. 242, emphasis added.

On March 20, 1980, there had been an earthquake on the volcano, of magnitude 4.2. By the end of April, the north side of the mountain had begun to bulge ominously. Then on May 18, there was another earthquake, this time of magnitude 5.1. The north side of the mountain collapsed. The resulting pyroclastic flow flattened trees and buildings over an area of 230 square miles. The most photographed and talked about volcanic eruption in history had begun.[11]

Why would creationists be interested in this event? It is because several things happened that model, as if in a laboratory, some of the processes that we think happened during the Flood. No one has done more research on the implications of the Mount St. Helens eruptions than Dr. Steve Austin, who has written innumerable scientific articles on the subject. This chapter can only contain some simplified overviews of his work, and the reader is referred to his numerous articles, as well as two popular level summaries of his ideas and a fascinating DVD, all of which are referenced.[12]

Austin's chapter in the *New Answers Book 3* includes a famous photo of him, standing at the foot of deposits on the North Fork of the Toutle River. The fine layering of the surfaces might suggest to an old-earth observer that the formation took thousands of years to form. Yet three distinct features have been dated, because we know exactly when they happened. The lowest layer formed in the initial explosion of May 18, 1980. The large 25-foot thick laminations were formed in three hours on June 12, 1980. Finally, the top deposit was overlain on March 19, 1982, at a subsequent eruption.

This latter 1982 eruption had other fascinating effects. The crater had filled with thick snow. This melted, creating a mudflow that eroded a canyon. The so-called Little Grand Canyon of the Toutle River is like a 1/40th scale model of the Grand Canyon of Arizona. It would seem likely, therefore, that

11. Both Mount St. Helens photos are courtesy of Wikimedia Commons.
12. Steven A. Austin, "Why Is Mount St. Helens Important to the Origins Controversy?" in Ken Ham, editor, *New Answers Book 3* (Green Forest, AR: Master Books, 2010), p. 253-262; John Morris and Steven A. Austin, *Footprints in the Ash* (Green Forest, AR: Master Books, 2003); *Mount St. Helens*, DVD, published by Compel Media, 2012.

such a flow at the end of the Flood, as the waters receded from the continents, could have caused large canyons.

The May 1980 eruption uprooted millions of trees. Many of these floated on nearby Spirit Lake. One remarkable feature of these logs is that they eventually began to float vertically, before sinking vertically into the newly formed sediment. Austin suggests that some 20,000 upright stumps were on the lake floor in August 1985.

In petrified forests, such as the one at Yellowstone, geologists have suggested that the upright logs were caused by thousands of years of growth and fossilization, yet have never been able to explain why many of these fossil trees have no root balls. Perhaps the truth is that these petrified logs did not grow *in situ*, but floated into position during the Flood, in a manner similar to the way that the logs behaved in Spirit Lake.

Lloyd Anderson operates a fascinating museum, called the 7 Wonders Creation Museum,[13] on the most popular access road to Mount St. Helens. He suggests that God has given us a reminder in these last days of how the Flood happened, so that we will deliver His message more effectively. If any readers get the opportunity to visit Washington State (or if you live there!) then I recommend visiting 7 Wonders and following one of Anderson's lectures and tours of the area.

Summary

There is no doubt in my mind that Christians owe a great debt of thanks to Drs. Whitcomb and Morris for their wonderful book *The Genesis Flood*. Generations of creationists have been inspired by that work to return to proclaiming the truth of God's Word from the very first verse. *The Genesis Flood* has also caused much research to be done, so that creationism is, today, in a healthy state, both theologically and scientifically. It is likely that those holding to a true biblical position will always be in a minority and always abused by skeptics and compromising Christians. Nevertheless, the history of creationism in the last 50 years is strong and is scientifically valid and credible.

---

13. 7 Wonders Creation Museum, 4749 Spirit Lake Highway, Silverlake, WA 98645, http://creationism.org/sthelens/index.htm, accessed 2/28/2012.

Chapter 8

How Did the Flood Start?

Part of the answer to this question is very easy. According to Genesis 7:11, the Flood was initiated by the "fountains of the deep" and "the windows of heaven."

> In the six hundredth year of Noah's life, in the second month, the seventeenth day of the month, on that day all the fountains of the great deep were broken up, and the windows of heaven were opened (Genesis 7:11).

The difficulty for the modern reader is in knowing exactly what these "fountains of the deep" and "windows of heaven" might be. Both phenomena are clearly important, so any explanation of how the Flood started must explain both phenomena. It could be inferred that the fountains are more fundamental than the windows. The explanation that I will pursue in this chapter will suggest that the windows of heaven were dependent on and caused by the fountains of the deep.

A Supernatural Event

There is a sense in which one instinctively feels that one should not look for naturalistic explanations for how the Flood started. It was, after all, a supernatural event. It was an event that had been prophesied beforehand. God had warned the people of the world in Genesis 6:3 and Enoch had prophesied the Flood in his prophetic naming of his son, Methuselah. Enoch's son's name, which some say means "his death shall bring it," and the Flood did indeed arrive the same year that Methuselah died.

Despite the supernatural nature of the event, it is not wrong to try to understand the mechanism by which God brought about this Flood. After all, God's creative acts had ended at the end of the creation week.

> Thus the heavens and the earth, and all the host of them, were finished. And on the seventh day God ended His work which He had done, and He rested on the seventh day from all His work which He had done. Then God blessed the seventh day and sanctified it, because in it He rested from all His work which God had created and made (Genesis 2:1–3).

We have a good chance of understanding anything that happened after Genesis 2:1–3 in terms of scientific processes, at least as far as we currently understand the necessary science — even if such understanding involves the knowledge that God suspended the normal scientific processes, as He did, for example, when Jesus walked on water in defiance of the law of gravity.

There is a difference between trying to understand a process like the Flood and trying to impose current scientific values on the Flood. If we do the former, we will start from what the Bible says, and our scientific understanding will be subservient to our understanding of Scripture. If we do the latter, then we look at current scientific processes and assume that such processes must have been the same in the past and at the same rate. This is the uniformitarian approach, which is particularly inappropriate when analyzing the Flood. It was the Apostle Peter who commented on such a methodology when he talked about the scoffers of the last days, who assume that "all things continue as *they were* from the beginning of creation," which is an error because "they willfully forget: that by the word of God the heavens were of old, and the earth standing out of water and in the water, by which the world that then existed perished, being flooded with water" (2 Peter 3:5–6). The Flood is, in fact, the great historical event that proves uniformitarianism to be wrong, and casts doubt on so much of modern-day ideas about historical science.[1]

---

1. I am using the term *historical science* here to refer to the opinions that some scientists produce about alleged one-of-a-kind events, which supposedly happened in the past and which cannot be repeated under laboratory conditions.

Creationist Scientific Models

A word needs to be included here about scientific models. I have written about the use of scientific models in creationism before, in a web article. In that article, I wrote:

> A scientific model does not have the same level of authority as Scripture. This is an important point, because there is always the danger that we will treat our scientific model as if it is Scripture, refusing ever to let go of it, and attacking those who question the model as if they were questioning Scripture.[2]

This fact is pertinent to any discussion on the Flood, as it is often found that a number of creationists have invested a lot of emotional capital into a particular scientific model and find it very difficult either to let go of it or to consider that they may have equated it with scriptural truth. One example of that, in this context, would be the vapor canopy theory (VCT), which I have analyzed elsewhere in this book. There is no doubt that there will be some readers who will be at the very least disappointed that I do not use that theory in order to explain how the Flood started. However, it does not seem to me — or, for that matter, to most serious creationists with scientific qualifications — that the VCT is adequate for explaining the scriptural truths. That does not mean, however, that I consider those who hold to VCT to be unscriptural. On the contrary, I know that they use their model precisely because they do want to adhere to Scripture. I hope that they will acknowledge that it is also not unscriptural to explain the Flood without VCT.

Catastrophic Plate Tectonics

The most viable model for how the Flood happened seems to me to be that known as catastrophic plate tectonics (CPT). This model has been around since about 1994, and has been refined and developed to a high level of sophistication. It has been written about and used by a galaxy of eminent creation scientists, many of whom are acknowledged experts in the field of geology. To mention some of their names might be dangerous for me, because I might miss some important pioneer, such is the level of expertise available among proponents of CPT. Five authors — Drs. Steven Austin, John Baumgardner, Russell Humphreys, Andrew Snelling, and

---

2. Paul F. Taylor, "Scriptural Truth and Scientific Models," 2011, www.creationtoday.org/scriptural-truth-and-scientific-models/, accessed 12/19/2011.

Kurt Wise — presented a paper at the Third International Conference on Creationism, Pittsburgh, Pennsylvania, July 18–23, 1994.[3] These authors have probably done as much if not more than anyone to develop the CPT model. Their paper has been the basis for much further research, most notably developed in Dr. Andrew Snelling's groundbreaking two-volume work, *Earth's Catastrophic Past*.[4] Much of the scientific work in this book owes a great deal to, and is strongly influenced by, Dr. Snelling's work.

In their paper, Austin et. al. gave a brief history of CPT, which really incorporates a history of plate tectonics in general. Even secular geologists note that the concept of plate tectonics owes much to the French 19th-century geologist Antonio Snider-Pellegrini (1802–1885). In 1858, Pellegrini published a book called *La Création et ses mystères dévoilés* ("Creation and Its Mysteries Unveiled"). In this book, he noted the remarkable similarity in shape between the coasts of Africa and South America — that they appeared to fit together like a jigsaw puzzle. See the world maps below.[5]

3. This paper has been reproduced in a number of places, most notably at the website of ICR: < http://static.icr.org/i/pdf/technical/Catastrophic-Plate-Tectonics-A-Global-Flood-Model.pdf >

4. Andrew A. Snelling, *Earth's Catastrophic Past* (Dallas, TX: Institute for Creation Research, 2009).

5. Illustration courtesy of http://en.wikipedia.org/wiki/File:Antonio_Snider-Pellegrini_Opening_of_the_Atlantic.jpg.

Pellegrini's thesis, therefore, was that at one time in the earth's history, all or most of the continents were joined together in one super-continent. His idea was that the continents had moved away from each other. This was an early version of the "continental drift" idea put forward by Alfred Wegener in 1927. Although Pellegrini did not use the term, the super-continent is often referred to as *Pangaea*.

For some reason, a small number of creationists have opposed the concept of continental drift. This may be because modern plate tectonic theory has become associated with long, slow processes and the concept of millions of years, which creationists rightly point out to be illogical and part of the program of the "scoffers" outlined in 2 Peter 3:4–5. For example, Dr. Walt Brown has criticized the Pangaea hypothesis in his book, *In the Beginning*. He claims that to make the "jigsaw" fit, Africa would have to be shrunk by 35 percent.[6] This is not the case, as can be seen from the following maps.[7]

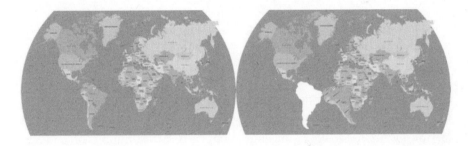

Pellegrini's ideas were not accepted in 1858. Another more influential book was published very shortly afterward. That book was Darwin's *Origin of Species*, in which the prevailing view of millions of years of slow processes was used. Pellegrini's ideas did not resonate with the times, because he believed the Bible to be true and assumed that this continental drift would have happened rapidly, in the early stages of the Flood. Referring to his own diagram, reproduced above, he said the following, which has been translated from the original French:

> The first, marked 9, or *before the separation*, shows our planet at the time of the interval, that is to say, from Adam to Noah, when

---

6. Walt Brown, *In the Beginning* (Phoenix, AZ: Center for Scientific Creation, 2008), 8th edition, Figure 51, < http://www.creationscience.com/onlinebook/HydroplateOverview4.html >, accessed 12/21/2011

7. Maps courtesy of vectorworldmap.com. The map on the right has been adapted for our illustration.

the land was still one piece traveled to the surface through gaps. In this period included the mass Atlantis [the term he gave to the pre-Flood Americas], which later give way to an ocean.[8]

Therefore, the CPT model falls completely within a biblical and creationist paradigm, and has, in recent years, become an excellent tool for explaining a large number of geological phenomena. What follows is only a layman's guide, a qualitative introduction to the CPT model. Those who wish to delve deeper into the science are invited to read the ICR reference given, and Andrew Snelling's important work.

A Pre-Flood Pangaea

On the third day of creation, God made dry land.

> Then God said, "Let the waters under the heavens be gathered together into one place, and let the dry land appear"; and it was so. And God called the dry land Earth, and the gathering together of the waters He called Seas. And God saw that it was good (Genesis 1:9–10).

If the waters were gathered together in one place, this would also suggest that the land was gathered in one place. Perhaps one can surmise that before the Flood there was more land than ocean. This would make sense, if we imagine that the post-Flood world needed to accommodate a greater amount of water. However, the issue about the relative amounts of land and sea are not important for the CPT model to work.

To reiterate, however, it would seem clear that there would probably have been just one continent before the Flood. Secular geologists coined the term *Pangaea* to describe this super-continent, during a symposium in 1927, which was meeting to discuss the continental drift theory, as described by Alfred Wegener in his book *The Origin of Continents and Oceans*, published in 1915.[9] These geologists believed in a vast age for the earth, but considering that the concept had been developed by Pellegrini, who, as we have seen, was a creationist, it seems appropriate and acceptable to refer to the pre-Flood continent as *Pangaea*.

---

8. Antonio Snider-Pellegrini, *La création et ses mystères dévoilés* (University of Michigan, 1858), retrieved December 21, 2011, p. 314, http://books.google.com/ebooks?id=yUBIAAAAMAAJ.

9. Willem A. J. M. van Waterschoot van der Gracht (and 13 other authors), *Theory of Continental Drift: a Symposium of the Origin and Movements of Land-masses of Both Inter-Continental and Intra-Continental, as Proposed by Alfred Wegener* (Tulsa, OK: The American Association of Petroleum Geologists & London: Thomas Murby & Co, 1928).

Runaway Subduction

Dating of rocks by secular means is an imprecise science, due to the assumptions that have to be made in order to calculate dates.[10] However, such secular dating methods can often give us the *relative* ages of rocks. By such means, we can see that present-day ocean basins are comprised of rocks that are younger than the rocks on the continents. Indeed, Baumgardner points out that "there is presently no ocean floor on the Earth that predates the deposition of the fossiliferous strata."[11] This suggests that all of the pre-Flood ocean basins have gone, and that all present-day ocean basins were formed during the Flood. As Baumgardner goes on to say, "In other words all the basalt that comprises the upper five kilometers or so of today's igneous ocean crust has cooled from the molten state since sometime after the Flood cataclysm began." This also suggests that runaway subduction might have been the engine that drove the rapid tectonic plate movement in the early days of the Flood.

Subduction is what happens when one tectonic plate moves under another. We see an effect like this at the boundary of the Nazca and South American plates, where the former is subducting under the latter. Under current time scales, this process is slow, but CPT theory suggests that this would have occurred rapidly at the beginning of the Flood. The reason for this suggestion is as follows. For reasons discussed later in the book, we are convinced that the overwhelming majority of fossils were laid down during the Flood. All modern ocean crust is younger than these fossils. Therefore, the ocean crust must have formed after the fossils; in other words, during the Flood. There must have been ocean crust before the Flood. None of this crust remains, so it must have been subducted. This subduction cannot have predated the Flood, so it must have all happened during the Flood. So subduction of the old crust and formation of new ocean crust both must have happened during the Flood, probably during the early stages. Therefore, both processes must have been rapid in the early days of the Flood. Such rapid subduction would have to have been a runaway process, and this runaway subduction becomes a neat explanation of what drove the Flood.

---

10. For further discussion on this point, see Mike Riddle, "Does Radiometric Dating Prove the Earth Is Old?" in Ken Ham, editor, *The New Answers Book 1* (Green Forest, AR: Master Books, 2006), p. 113–124.

11. John R. Baumgardner, "Runaway Subduction as the Driving Mechanism for the Genesis Flood," 1994, http://www.icr.org/research/index/researchp_jb_runawaysubduction/.

Returning to the relevant passage of Scripture, we read again:

> On that day all the *fountains of the great deep were broken up, and the windows of heaven were opened* (Genesis 7:11, emphasis added).

Two things occurred to initiate the Flood, which were probably related. The phrases "fountains of the deep" and "windows of heaven" would seem to be euphemisms. That is to say they are phrases that are, at the same time, poetic and yet also referring to literal phenomena. The concept of "fountains of the deep" would seem to imply sources of water that are deep down in the earth. CPT theory would suggest that the earth's mantle would be the principle source of this water. This water could have come to the surface if some of the crust were broken.

We would suggest that the breaking of the crust would have happened in the ocean basin, so that the pre-Flood crust began to be split into plates. Pre-Flood oceanic crust would have to move somewhere, especially if new crust material was being produced somewhere around ridges like the Mid-Atlantic Ridge. Since the oceanic crust is heavier than the continental crust, it would probably tend to subduct under a continental plate.

The breaking up of the ocean crust would bring water into contact with a hot mantle. This water would be superheated to temperatures well above the boiling point of water ($100°C$, $212°F$). This superheated water would be thrown high into the atmosphere at supersonic speeds. We must remember that whatever process God used to initiate the Flood must have been dramatic, because the Flood was the single most important geological event of the world, other than creation. The superheated supersonic jets of water would eventually fall, and it is suggested that this effect is what the Bible is referring to when it talks about "the windows of heaven." Additionally, more water would have become available from the mantle, so that there would easily be enough water to flood the entire globe. Where that water went after the Flood is a question for a later chapter.

This breaking up of the oceanic crust would have had physical effects farther down in the earth. The water would have caused cooling of the mantle. This cooling and the subduction of oceanic crust into the mantle would have cooled the outer core of the earth. Since this is the most likely engine of the earth's magnetic field, such cooling could have caused rapid and frequent reversals of the magnetic field. There will be more on the implications of this shortly.

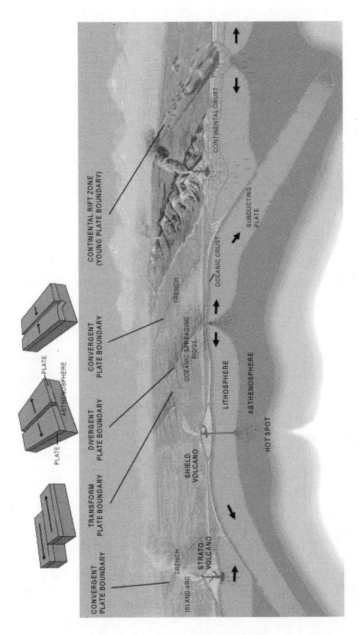

This is a good example of a continental rift zone.

(Cross section by José F. Vigil from *This Dynamic Planet*; produced jointly by the U.S. Geological Survey, the Smithsonian Institution, and the U.S. Naval Research Laboratory)

Here is where CPT theory makes a remarkable prediction. Before we visit this prediction, we should remember the logical status of the outcome of a prediction. A fulfilled theoretical prediction does not prove a theory — it can only disprove a theory. For example, if it were an inevitable corollary of a theory that the sky is blue, and we do indeed observe that the sky is blue, this does not prove the theory — it is merely consistent with the theory. There could be alternative explanations as to why the sky is blue. If our theory predicted that the sky is green, however, and we note that the sky is blue, then we have proved our theory wrong.

So this gives us the opportunity to look at a prediction that CPT theory can make. If the pre-Flood ocean plate were subducted into the mantle, and this occurred rapidly a mere 4,400 years ago, then there should be remains of such a plate.

Secular geologists have also used the concept of subduction as an engine to drive plate tectonics. For example, Conrad et al have proposed precisely this mechanism in an article entitled "How Mantle Slabs Drive Plate Tectonics."[12] In this article, slabs are assumed to be subducted portions of former tectonic plates. Conrad shows that the existence of such slabs is suggested by data collected in seismic surveys. Analysis of seismic waves can produce an "image" of the mantle, in a manner analogous to ultrasonic scanning. Conrad's evidence suggests a slab in the vicinity of the Pacific Ring of Fire. The image shown is produced by a computer model used by NASA but that suggests the existence of a subducted ocean plate, known as the Farallon Plate, which geologists assume was subducted under the North American plate.

What the secular geologic model cannot account for, however, is the continued existence of slabs, such as the Farallon Plate, if they are millions of years old. Their existence suggests both a recent and catastrophic mode for their existence, and is more in line with CPT than with conventional plate tectonics.

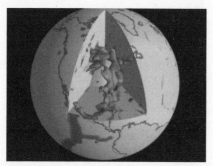
Farallon Plate

Symmetrical Magnetic Striping

With interesting evidence for the runaway subduction of the pre-Flood oceanic crust existing, we now turn to evidence for the creation of new oceanic crust.

---

12. C.P. Conrad et al, *Science* 298, 207 (2002); DOI: 10.1126/science. 1074161.

CPT, like conventional plate tectonics, proposes that new oceanic crust would have formed at ridges, such as the Mid-Atlantic Ridge. New material emerging through this ridge would spread outward as the plates move apart. Such new material contains magnetic fragments. In a molten medium, these magnets are able to align themselves with the earth's magnetic field. However, if that field changes direction, after the material has solidified, then the magnets will not be able to realign themselves in the solid matrix and will act as a sort of "fossil" of an earlier magnetic field.

If the African and South American plates had always moved apart at the present slow rate, then any magnetic material would have been arranged randomly, as the earth's field altered. However, we have already seen that CPT predicts a rapid and frequent reversing of the earth's magnetic field. If we couple this prediction with the idea that these plates moved away rapidly, as the Mid-Atlantic Ridge made material rapidly, then the magnetic reversals would be symmetric. New material would spread from the ridge and solidify, then the field would change and more material would spread out on both east and west sides of the ridge, with the magnets aligned opposite. So, if CPT is correct, there should be "stripes" of alternating magnetic material symmetrically arranged on either side of the ridge. However, if conventional plate tectonics is right, the existence of such symmetric stripes would be harder to explain.

In fact, the Mid-Atlantic Ridge does exhibit the symmetric magnetic striping predicted by CPT.[13]

Summary

In this chapter, we have suggested that the theory known as Catastrophic Plate Tectonics seems to be the best modern model of how the Flood began. The model includes a sensible suggestion as to the nature of the "fountains of the deep" and "the windows of heaven" and suggests an engine that could have driven the early stages of the Flood. The model utilizes the conventional hypotheses of Pangaea and plate tectonics. We have also seen that there is much scientific evidence, which is best explained by using the CPT model.

---

13. Andrew A. Snelling, *Earth's Catastrophic Past* (Dallas, TX: Institute for Creation Research, 2009), p. 696–698.

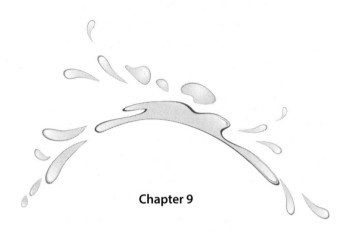

Chapter 9

The Waters Above

Creationists have been referring to the Flood for a long time. Their commendable desire to proclaim that the Flood was a real, global event has led to some problematic interpretations of Scripture. This chapter is about one of these, and is likely to be one of the more controversial chapters in this book, as it may offend some fellow creationists. At stake is my contention that the biblical phrase "waters above" does not refer to a vapor canopy at the edge of the atmosphere, and that some creationists have elevated what was merely a scientific model to the status of biblical inerrancy.

The Canopy Theory in a Nutshell

The *canopy theory* is an honorable attempt to interpret Scripture correctly, and also to account for the waters of the Flood. The theory starts with day 2 of the creation week.

> Then God said, "Let there be a firmament in the midst of the waters, and let it divide the waters from the waters." Thus God made the firmament, and divided the waters which were under the firmament from the waters which were above the firmament; and it was so. And God called the firmament Heaven. So the evening and the morning were the second day (Genesis 1:6–8).

This passage is clearly talking about the creation of a *firmament* and the division of waters into waters above and below the firmament. The basis of the canopy theory is that the firmament represents the earth's atmosphere and the waters above are in the form of a canopy, which surrounded the earth before the Flood. It is thought that this canopy could have been the source, or at least *a* source, for the waters of the Flood. The Flood would, therefore, have been initiated by the collapse of this canopy. It is thought that the pre-Flood canopy would have caused conditions of environment and weather before the Flood to be very different from those of today. The actual nature of the canopy differs in competing interpretations, with some assuming it to be a canopy of water vapor and others suggesting a crystalline canopy. It must be emphasized that many creationists, myself included, have held to and taught the canopy theory in the past. In quoting a number of great creationist writers who have held to the canopy theory, it must not be thought that I am intending to be disrespectful of their position. My rejection of their support for the canopy theory is merely an indication that our understanding moves on, and should not be taken to imply anything other than the immense respect that I have for such men.

Primary among these has to be the late Dr. Henry Morris, the father of modern creationism. In his wonderful book *The Genesis Record*, he said:

> The "waters above the firmament" thus probably constituted a vast blanket of water vapor above the troposphere and possibly above the stratosphere as well, in the high-temperature region now known as the ionosphere, and extending far into space.[1]

Dr. Morris went on to list some of the ways in which a vapor canopy might have made pre-Flood conditions different from today. These include:

- uniform world temperatures
- uniform warmth
- prevention of cosmic radiation, leading to longer pre-Flood life spans
- uniform worldwide moisture, with no deserts or ice caps

In 1976, Morris was satisfied that such a vapor canopy would provide the water required for the Flood.

> A worldwide rain lasting forty days would be quite impossible under present atmospheric conditions; so this phenomenon required

---

1. Henry Morris, *The Genesis Record* (Grand Rapids, MI: Baker Book House, 1976), p. 59.

an utterly different source of atmospheric waters than now obtains. This we have already seen to be the "waters above the firmament," the vast thermal blanket of invisible water vapor that maintained the greenhouse effect in the antediluvian world. These waters somehow were to condense and fall on the earth.[2]

The *vapor canopy model* was the most common canopy model among creationists, and was the one I taught in my own presentations for many years. Some creationists, however, have suggested a canopy of ice. Carl Baugh, for example, suggests a "crystalline canopy."[3] In this theory, the ice would be made of either ice crystals or of a solid, metallic hydrogen lattice, suspended above the atmosphere by the magnetic levitation. This specific crystalline canopy has particular problems. Magnetic levitation would not work on molecules like water or hydrogen, where paramagnetic properties dominate over diamagnetic properties. Also, a solid lattice of ice would make it difficult or impossible to see stars. Finally, hydrogen can only exhibit metallic properties under extreme conditions of high pressure and temperatures near absolute zero. Therefore, the crystalline lattice theory need not detain us further.

Problems with the Canopy Theory

A number of significant scientific problems have come to light that cast doubt on the canopy theory.

Canopy theorists have used the canopy concept to explain a number of pre-Flood effects. For example, they have suggested that the canopy would have increased atmospheric pressure at the earth's surface. Genesis 6 refers to "giants," and it is suggested that humans would not have been able to grow to giant height without increased pressure. However, giant height of seven or eight feet is completely feasible with normal atmospheric pressure. Canopy theorists have also claimed that the giant insects seen in the fossil record would not have been able to breathe without increased oxygen partial pressure. Again, this can be shown not to be the case. Indeed, increased oxygen partial pressure can actually be shown to have a deleterious effect on the longevity of humans.

On the subject of longevity, it has been suggested that the longevity of humans before the Flood was due to greater atmospheric pressure. However,

2. Ibid., p. 191.
3. C.E. Baugh, *Crystalline Canopy Theory*, http://184.154.224.5/~creatio1/index.php?option=com_content&task=view&id=74&Itemid=29 (undated document), accessed 01/06/2012.

a better explanation is the comparative absence of mutations among the human gene pool. The level of mutations would have greatly increased after the Flood, so this could explain the rapid decrease in longevity.

Scientist Dr. Larry Vardiman has taken a close interest in the canopy theory, having calculated many different models for how it could have worked. To the best of my knowledge, he is still wedded to a version of the canopy theory. Nevertheless, his research has pointed out a number of problems with the theory.

It must be remembered that water vapor is probably the most significant of the so-called greenhouse gases. So any vapor canopy would trap more heat from the sun, leading to increased temperatures at the earth's surface. Vardiman's computer models showed that "any canopy containing more than about 20 inches (51 cm) of water produced such a strong greenhouse effect that surface temperatures became unsuitable for life."[4] Vardiman proposed that cirrus clouds near the top of the canopy could have helped against this effect, but other researchers, such as Snelling, have suggested that these would insufficiently mitigate against the problems caused by the canopy.

Clearly, 20 inches of water is insufficient to explain the water of the Flood. However, even if further factors are introduced, to allow the canopy to increase in size, it is still only possible to produce a canopy that would deposit a little more than 3 feet (1 m) of water on the earth. Some creationists have suggested that the canopy would not therefore be the only source of water. This indeed makes sense. My chapter on catastrophic plate tectonics shows that the major source of water would probably have been the mantle. But if no canopy can be proposed that would represent a significant percentage of the water required for the Flood, one wonders why one needs a canopy theory at all, especially as we now move on to some scriptural objections to the canopy theory. These arguments are significant. If a few scientific results looked problematic, but we could show that Scripture clearly taught a canopy, then we would know that the scientific results were currently incomplete, and we would trust Scripture. However, I will now show that the canopy is not required by Scripture, and is even probably incorrect according to Scripture.

Dr. Russell Humphreys has suggested a cosmology, based on the stretching of space.[5] In this cosmology, Humphreys has suggested that the

---

4. Andrew A. Snelling, *Earth's Catastrophic Past* (Dallas, TX: Institute for Creation Research, 2009), p. 667.
5. Larry Vardiman and D. R. Humphreys. 2010. "A New Creationist Cosmology: In No Time at All," Part 1, *Acts & Facts* 39 (11) (2010): 12–15.

firmament, which divides the waters above from the waters below in Genesis 1:6–8, represents the stretching of the universe. The Hebrew word translated *firmament* is *râqîya* (עיקר). This word has a similar root to the concept of "stretching" metal by hammering it. Some versions translate the word as *expanse.* Humphreys therefore uses this concept to explain the various red shift measurements observed in space. However, a side effect of his theory is that the "waters above" would therefore be beyond the stars, rather than at the edge of the atmosphere. This makes sense for a number of reasons.

First, we read in Genesis 1 that the sun, moon, and stars were made *in* the firmament (Genesis 1:15). If there were a canopy at the edge of the atmosphere, this would mean that the stars were *above* the canopy, which is not what Scripture says.

Second, some have pointed to birds flying in the canopy as pointing to the canopy being at the edge of the atmosphere. However, if the canopy were at the edge of the universe, this would not contradict this verse (Genesis 1:20). Moreover, the Hebrew actually talks about the "face of the firmament." Some versions, such as the NKJV, refer to this: "Let birds fly above the earth across the face of the firmament of the heavens." So the birds are not actually *in* the firmament but flying across the face of it.

Third, Psalm 148:4 shows that the "waters above" are still actually in place, because this psalm was written after the Flood. That would also suggest that the "waters above" had nothing to do with the Flood, and lends support to Humphreys' idea that the "waters above" are beyond the last galaxies, not at the edge of the atmosphere.

It has been hard for many modern creationists to let go of the vapor canopy theory. I had similar emotions. Nevertheless, we must face the fact that the canopy theory was not Scripture, but rather a scientific model to aid our understanding. Modern scientific and scriptural understandings both show that the canopy model is not necessary. It seems today that the effects, for which the canopy theory was developed to explain, are actually better explained by other means.

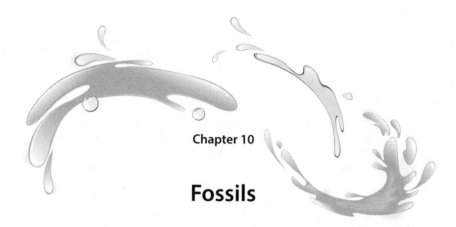

Chapter 10

Fossils

F ossils are evidence for evolution. We know this, right? That's fact! Isn't it? You might well suppose so if you read the high school textbooks. A famous British biology textbook by D.G. Mackean says this:

> The evidence from the fossil record supports the theory of evolution because it shows animals and plants becoming more varied and more complicated as time goes on.[1]

This is a common statement, and widely believed. It is taught in high school biology on both sides of the Atlantic. On closer analysis, however, the statement does not say exactly what presuppositions are being made. One popular dictionary rightly defines *fossil record* as "the totality of fossils, both discovered and undiscovered, and their placement in *fossiliferous* (fossil-containing) rock formations and sedimentary layers (strata)."[2] This definition of the totality of fossils as the fossil record does not contain any connotations about how the fossils may have come to exist. Yet the above textbook statement contains the phrase "as time goes on." The implication is that the fossil record itself can give a measure of the passage of time. This is not correct. To assume this to be true would be a circular argument. It is

---

1. D.G. Mackean, *GCSE Biology* (London, England: John Murray, 2000), p. 210.
2. Wikipedia definition, *Fossils*, http://en.wikipedia.org/wiki/Fossil_record, accessed 1/23/2012, emphasis original.

logical to say that *if* evolution were true, including the time scale required, *then* one might expect the fossil record to appear in the way it does. But it is illogical to make the reverse argument, if there is any possibility of an alternative explanation as to how the fossil record was produced. And there is indeed a highly sophisticated, yet simply based, alternative explanation. The textbook statement above starts with the presupposition that the fossil record was produced over long periods of time, amounting to millions of years. The alternative creationist explanation, which will be detailed later in this chapter, starts with the logical presupposition that the majority of the fossil record was formed in the Flood.

Does the Fossil Record Show Change over Time?

The idea that the fossil record shows change over time presupposes that the fossil record took long periods of time to form. Creationists reject that presupposition. However, in order to prove a point, let us temporarily suspend our rejection, and suppose that the fossil record did indeed take millions of years to form. If it did, does it really show evidence of change over time?

Once we have temporarily accepted Mackean's presupposition on time, we realize that there is a second presupposition in his statement. If, as Mackean suggests, organisms have become more complicated, it presupposes that earlier organisms were less complicated. The evolutionary presupposition of time in the fossil record is that, generally speaking, lower strata represent earlier periods of time. The organisms in these strata can therefore be assumed to be less complicated than those in the higher strata. Therefore, a trilobite is less complicated than a mammoth.

Evolutionists assume that a trilobite is not too dissimilar from a modern creature such as a woodlouse. Is a woodlouse less complicated, therefore, than an elephant? If we look at the chemicals contained within these creatures, the complexity within the woodlouse is just as great as that within an elephant. If we look at cell structure under a microscope, we will see that the structures within a woodlouse are just as complicated as those within elephants. The same would be true for other "simple" organisms, such as worms or snails. Dr. Vij Sodera says this:

> Like modern horseshoe crabs, trilobites would have had hearts to pump their blood, a well-defined brain and nervous system, and would have been able to periodically shed their shells (*carapaces*) to enable them to grow. The eyes and limbs were all very well developed.

Virtually all the enzymes, proteins, internal organs, muscle systems, etc. found in living animals would have been represented in this (supposedly) ancient and "primitive" animal. And yet it is supposed to have developed all this sophistication and originated some 500 million years ago.[3]

In a lengthy chapter on the fossil record, Dr. Sodera catalogs a large number of such anomalies — supposedly ancient animals showing great complexity, and so-called simpler animals existing after the "more complicated" types, into which we would have expected them to evolve. For example, it might be supposed that bony fish would have evolved from cartilaginous fish, yet there is no reason to suppose that sharks (which are cartilaginous) are less complicated than, say, salmon. Similarly, mammalian evolution is presumed to have proceeded by placental mammals having evolved from marsupials, and marsupials from monotremes (of which the only two modern examples are the platypus and the echidna). Yet the earliest known monotreme fossil is supposedly 2 million years old, whereas the supposedly oldest known mammal is the *morganucodon*, which seems to be a shrew-like creature. If monotremes — which are supposedly simpler than placentals — were the ancestors of all mammals, then it must surely, at one time, have represented a large number of species. Where are all the fossils of these species?

It is a fascinating study to examine the many fossils that are recognizable. This picture shows a fossil of *Palaeobatrachus gigas*, which is a type of frog. For fun, I often show this picture[4] during my talks and ask them how they know that this fossil is a frog. Many people look puzzled at that point, until someone is brave enough to say, "Because it looks like a frog!"

If it looks like a frog, and we suspect it hops like a frog and croaks like a frog, then the chances are that it may well be Kermit's cousin! Contrary to Mackean's statement, the fossil record does not illustrate an upward change in complexity. Dr. Sodera quotes L.B. Halstead — very much a hostile witness!

3. Vij Sodera, *One Small Speck to Man: The Evolution Myth* (Vija Sodera Productions, 2009), 2nd edition, p. 46.
4. http://commons.wikimedia.org/wiki/File:Fossilised_frog.jpg

The silverfish . . . survived since the early Devonian [345–395 mya]. . . . The cockroach remained unchanged since the Carboniferous [280–345mya]. . . .[5]

I have in my collection pictures of many fossilized creatures that look identical to modern creatures, and I like to use these in my talks, comparing fossil heart urchins, frogs, and sea lilies with their modern counterparts, to show that there is no change. The fossil record, therefore, is not a record of change, as Mackean suggests and as so many high school biology texts suggest. Rather it is a record of two things — *stasis*: the fact that so many organisms have hardly changed at all, and *extinction*: the fact that there are some animals in the fossil record that don't appear to be around anymore. In no way does the fossil record appear to be a record of evolutionary change.

The second presupposition of Mackean's statement has therefore been shown to be incorrect, and we can now move on to show that the presupposition of long periods of time is also not sensible.

Fossilization Occurs Quickly

Most paleontologists today accept that fossilization *can* occur quickly, though they will not normally admit that it is usually a rapid process. Indeed, the impression is still given by many — especially by high school science teachers — that fossilization is, in fact, a slow process. The following description is taken from the National Park Service website, and describes fossilization at the Dinosaur National Monument near Vernal, Utah.

> Scientists believe that at one time, about 150 million years ago, the river dried up during a drought. The last watering hole was located where the Quarry Visitor Center is today. As the watering hole vanished, the dinosaurs died. Their carcasses were scattered about the dried riverbed. After the drought ended, the river again began to flow. Over time, dinosaur bones were buried under sand and gravel, and the fossilization process began.
>
> As ages passed, that river vanished. Other rivers and seas came and went, leaving layer after layer of sand and mud that slowly solidified into rock. As water seeping through the ground filled the buried bones with dissolved silica, they became rock hard.[6]

---

5. L.B. Halstead, *Hunting the Past* (London: Hamish Hamilton, 1982), p. 196–197, quoted in Sodera, *One Small Speck to Man*, p. 51.
6. http://www.nps.gov/history/museum/exhibits/dino/douglas.html, accessed 1/23/2012.

Roger Patterson, in his excellent book *Evolution Exposed: Earth Science*, analyzes the above claim thus:

> This is a nice story, but that is not how fossils form, let alone a layer 50 feet thick. Organisms must be buried quickly in an environment that lacks oxygen in order to be fossilized. If they are not, scavengers and bacteria will quickly decompose the organisms. The most common fossils at the site are freshwater clams. Most of these clam shells are found opened, showing that they were buried after death. However, some of the clams are found still closed, indicating that they were buried while still alive. The clams could not have been buried alive if the river and waterhole had dried up.[7]

There are many examples of fossils, the appearance of which immediately suggest rapid burial. Fossilized tracks are fairly common. If the fossilization of these was not rapid, then the tracks would soon have been washed away, or erased by other animal tracks. Sometimes, soft-bodied creatures, such as jellyfish, are found fossilized. These creatures will often "disappear" in a matter of hours, if stranded on a beach. Yet fossilized jellyfish are not rare.

A creature trapped in wet concrete would be "fossilized" quickly. On an evolutionary time scale, it is often assumed that time and pressure forms the rock. In practice, it is more likely that the rock formation, or solidification, is a chemical process, like the hardening of cement.

Polystrate Fossils

One of the most remarkable examples of rapid fossilization must be the polystrate fossil. These are fossils that straddle more than one layer of strata. Many of these fossils are trees or other large plants, such as lycopods. In most other areas, the great thicknesses of the rock layers and the existence of multiple layers would suggest time periods of millions of years to the long-age secular geologist. Therefore, the existence of polystrate fossils is very difficult for such long-agers to explain.

The editor of the relevant Wikipedia page has referenced Gastaldo in order to suggest that some trees continued to grow while being gradually surrounded by sediment.[8] Explanations of this sort stretch credulity to the

---

7. R. Patterson, *Evolution Exposed: Earth Science* (Hebron, KY: Answers in Genesis, 2008), p. 149–150.
8. Wikipedia article on "Polystrate Fossils," http://en.wikipedia.org/wiki/Polystrate_fossils, R.A. Gastaldo, "Regenerative Growth in Fossil Horsetails (Calamites) Following Burial by Alluvium," *Historical Biology*, 6(3) (1992): 203–220.

limit. Other long-age geologists concede that the polystrate fossils must have been formed rapidly, but maintain that the catastrophe that formed them must have been local in nature. Derek Ager, a secular geologist at the University of Swansea, has studied polystrate fossils in carboniferous (coal-bearing) rocks in South Wales. He has concluded that the formation of these fossils must have been very rapid. He says:

> Probably the most convincing proof of the local rapidity of terrestrial sedimentation is provided by the presence in the coal measures of trees still in position of life.[9]

What such uniformitarian geologists do not address is the appearance of geological age seen in the surrounding strata. If these strata are the result of rapid and catastrophic deposition, as Ager suggests, then why does this mechanism not apply to other locations where similarly scaled collections of strata are situated?

Michael Oard and Hank Giesecke wrote an impressive summary of the issues surrounding polystrate fossils for the *Creation Research Society Quarterly*, while reporting on research they had undertaken at a number of coal mines in Alaska. They favor a model that has been discussed by other creationists that these trees may have dropped vertically through water from floating log mats.

> This type of deposition of vegetation fits the evidence found at the open-pit coal mines in Alaska. For instance, leaf litter from both deciduous and evergreen trees is abundant along some bedding planes and shows little or no decay. Rapid sedimentation would also be required to preserve this litter.[10]

Oard and Giesecke report that, in one example, whose photograph is included in their paper, "The tree seems to have pushed the strata downward," noting:

> This would be unlikely if the trees grew in place. However, if the trees sank from a floating log mat, then soft strata would have been depressed into a bowl shape upon impact.[11]

---

9. Derek Ager, *The New Catastrophism — The Importance of the Rare Event in Geological History* (Cambridge, UK: Cambridge University Press, 1993), p. 47.
10. Michael J. Oard and Hank Giesecke, "Polystrate Fossils Require Rapid Deposition," *Creation Research Society Quarterly* 43(4) (2006): 232–240.
11. Ibid.

Polystrate fossils are very common, especially, but not exclusively, in carboniferous sediments. Their existence is clearly very difficult to explain by secular, long-age geology, but very consistent with the idea of sediments being laid down rapidly during a worldwide Flood.

The Geologic Column

A great deal has been written by creationists on the subject of the geologic column. Our criticism of the geologic column is one of our strong suits, as creationists! Therefore, this analysis can really only scratch the surface of what has been written.

The geologic column collects classification of the earth's rocks, according to a secular geologic time scale. In its revision guide for teenagers, the BBC describes it thus:

> The geological periods relate to events which have happened in the earth's history. For example, during the *carboniferous period* there were tropical weather conditions in the United Kingdom, and coal and limestone were formed.
>
> The most recent period in geological time is called the *quaternary*, when the Ice Age occurred.
>
> Rocks are formed at different times, and are a result of the environment present during that time. For example, chalk is formed in the *cretaceous* period, as this is when warm tropical seas were present around the shores of the United Kingdom.[12]

The classic geologic column is said to be comprised of ten geologic systems. These are Cambrian, Ordovician, Silurian, Devonian, Carboniferous, Permian, Triassic, Jurassic, Cretaceous, and Tertiary. Dr. Steve Austin has written a very useful article on the website of the Institute for Creation Research, in which he lists *Ten Misconceptions about the Geologic Column*.[13] All of his points are worth reading, and it is relevant to repeat some of them here. Austin starts his article by reminding us that the geologic column was not, in fact, devised to include millions of years of supposed geologic history. In fact, the people who originated the idea of the geologic column were actually creationists!

---

12. BBC Bitesize, http://www.bbc.co.uk/schools/gcsebitesize/geography/rock_landscapes/geological_time_rev1.shtml, accessed 1/23/2012.
13. Steven A. Austin, *Ten Misconceptions about the Geologic Column*, http://www.icr.org/article/ten-misconceptions-about-geologic-column/, accessed 1/23/2012.

It may sound surprising, but the standard geologic column was devised before 1860 by catastrophists who were creationists. Adam Sedgewick, Roderick Murchison, William Coneybeare, and others affirmed that the earth was formed largely by catastrophic processes, and that the earth and life were created. These men stood for careful empirical science and were not compelled to believe evolutionary speculation or side with uniformitarian theory. Although most would be called "progressive creationists" in today's terminology, they would not be pleased to see all the evolutionary baggage that has been loaded onto their classification of strata.[14]

The label of some of the geologic layers is interesting. One layer is known as Tertiary, and the newer rock being formed today is known as Quaternary. These terms mean third and fourth, respectively. Where are the first and second — the Primary and Secondary rocks? Originally, early geologists referred to rocks that they thought had been created during the creation week as Primary, and rocks formed during the Flood as Secondary. Thus, Tertiary rocks were formed after the Flood, and Quaternary more recently. So the very names given to these classifications remind us of the original scriptural nature of this study.

There are some people who have said, with certain justification, that the geologic column only exists in textbooks. Anti-creationist writers have wanted to jump on such statements by claiming that the entire geologic column exists in some parts of the world. This is not, in fact, the case. What is true is that there are a small number of places where all ten systems can be found in order. For example, Glen Morton has claimed that the entire column exists in North Dakota.[15] This claim is somewhat disingenuous, however. Each of the ten systems listed above is highly complex, containing subdivisions that are not all present in North Dakota, nor in the other places that Austin lists as having all ten systems (west Nepal, west Bolivia, and central Poland). Austin goes on to show that each individual system is incomplete in these areas, so they cannot be used to justify the existence of the whole geologic column. Moreover, as we will see later, there is a much simpler explanation for the ordering of rock layers than the evolutionary explanation. Austin also points out that there are areas in the world where the systems are in the wrong order. This is justified by alluding to "overthrusts" — the idea that older rock has been pushed over

---

14. Ibid.
15. Glen Morton, *The Geologic Column and Its Implications to the Flood*, http://home.entouch. net/dmd/geo.htm, 2007, accessed 1/23/2012.

the top of younger rock. Yet we have no good mechanism for how this could happen, and it is really only an explanation born out of desperation.

It is supposed that the geologic column gives us the ages of various fossils. In fact, the usual method of dating a rock is to see what sort of fossils the rock contains. If the rock contains fossils that are 100 million years old, then the rock is 100 million years old. The fossils must be 100 million years old, because they are contained in rock that is 100 million years old.[16] It is often claimed that independent dating of rocks is available by radiometric dating. This is also not the case. Radiometric dating is carried out on igneous rocks, whereas fossils are found in sedimentary rocks. Of course, igneous rocks adjacent to the sedimentary rock under observation could be dated radiometrically. However, it also needs to be noted that radiometric dating is based on a number of assumptions. These assumptions, and other problematic issues regarding radiometric dating, are discussed in another chapter.

The geologic column was not compiled due to independent dating of the rocks, however. The column was constructed before radiometric dating was developed. Old-earth geologists looked at current rates of deposition of sediment and measured the thicknesses of sediments, and then, by using uniformitarian assumptions, the millions of years that they thought would be needed to build each sediment layer were estimated. Even today, radiometric dates will be "calibrated" against the "known" dates of rocks, in order to eliminate the many occasions when a raw radiometric calculation would give a date that does not fit in with the preconceived opinions on how old the rocks are supposed to be.

A Flood Model for Fossilization

So far, we have seen that the slow, evolutionary time scale for fossilization is not correct; that the geologic column cannot be used to suggest ages of fossils; and that the fossil record does not illustrate evolutionary changes. These have all been necessary negative analyses of the evolutionary view of fossils. However, it would now be fair to ask what positive statements we can make. It is clear that a Flood model to explain fossils will have to explain how fossilization could occur rapidly. It will also have to explain why certain fossils are usually found in certain layers — an observation that evolutionists have presented as a clinching "proof" for their beliefs. As we will observe, a detailed Flood model has been developed to explain the layering of fossils. This model is both highly sophisticated and yet simple to understand, as all

---

16. Henry M. Morris, "Circular Reasoning in Evolutionary Biology," http://www.icr.org/article/circular-reasoning-evolutionary-biology/, accessed 1/23/2012.

the best theories should be. It is also capable of easily explaining the various out-of-place fossils that exist around the world, so this makes it a much more powerful explanation than the evolutionary model.

A common accusation made by evolutionists against creationists is to ask why we cannot find fossilized rabbits in Jurassic rock. The assumption is that if we reject the evolutionary explanation of the geologic column, then we must reject the actual reality of the geologic column. This is not the case, and the question completely misses the point. The reality of the layering of rocks, and the positioning of fossils within these layers, is not in question. It is the evolutionary explanation of that layering that is rejected, and the concept that great depth of strata represents millions of years of rock formation.

This diagram is typical of the way that the geologic column is represented in textbooks. The following version is based on a similar one from the Dinosaur National Monument's website.[17]

Two things need to be explained about graphics like this. The first is that, as we have previously discussed, such a diagram is actually a composite from observations made in various parts of the world. The second point to make is more subtle.

The illustrations of creatures in the column do not suggest that those creatures are only found in those strata. Instead, in an evolutionary model, the illustration merely gives the "first" appearance of those creatures. For example, nautiloids are not found below the Ordovician, but they *are* found above the Ordovician. A quick search of the web will turn up nautiloid fossils from the Jurassic. A first sight of a column such as this might lead one to suppose that no marine fossils are found in the upper strata. That is not the case. Marine fossils occur throughout the geologic column.

Nevertheless, there are some well-known observations that are beyond dispute. Among these is the fact that we do not find dinosaur fossils along with those of well-known modern-type mammals.[18] We do, however, find dinosaur fossils mostly with gymnosperm plants. Similarly, mammalian fossils are found in strata with angiosperms (flowering plants).

An evolutionary interpretation of the geologic column leads one to suppose that much of the world at the time of the dinosaurs would have had a common climate and ecosystem, involving the same sorts of plants. Yet, in

---

17. http://www.nps.gov/history/museum/exhibits/dino/geotime/geotime2.html.
18. This is not the place to get into controversies over whether there are any examples, for instance, of dinosaur fossils along with fossilized human remains. Even if such examples were verified, they would be the exception rather than the general rule, and would be easily explained by the model being described here.

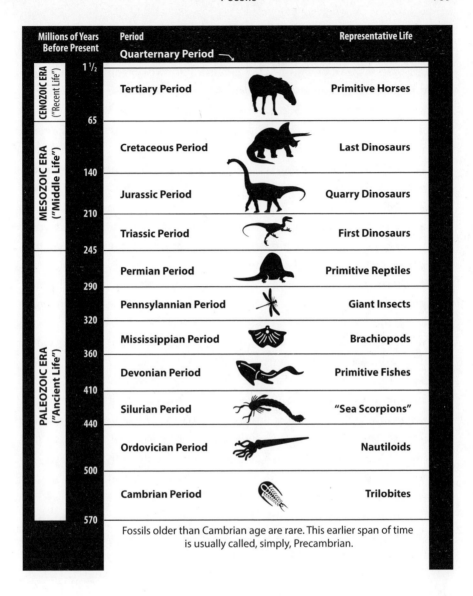

Millions of Years Before Present	Period		Representative Life
	Quarternary Period		
CENOZOIC ERA ("Recent Life") — 1 ½	**Tertiary Period**		**Primitive Horses**
65			
MESOZOIC ERA ("Middle Life")	**Cretaceous Period**		**Last Dinosaurs**
140	**Jurassic Period**		**Quarry Dinosaurs**
210	**Triassic Period**		**First Dinosaurs**
245	**Permian Period**		**Primitive Reptiles**
PALEOZOIC ERA ("Ancient Life") — 290	**Pennsylannian Period**		**Giant Insects**
320	**Mississippian Period**		**Brachiopods**
360	**Devonian Period**		**Primitive Fishes**
410	**Silurian Period**		**"Sea Scorpions"**
440	**Ordovician Period**		**Nautiloids**
500	**Cambrian Period**		**Trilobites**
570			

Fossils older than Cambrian age are rare. This earlier span of time is usually called, simply, Precambrian.

today's world, we have a wide variety of ecosystems. The model that many creationists have suggested makes far more sense. It proposes that dinosaurs are not found in the same strata as mammals, because dinosaurs and mammals did not generally live in the same ecosystems. In other words, in the world before the Flood, the pre-Flood supercontinent, which we described in the chapter on the Flood mechanism, would have had much local variety of ecosystems. We therefore see the strata not as distinct and different eras, but as distinct and different geographical localities. Because this present work is a layman's guide, we will make some simplified general points about these local ecosystems, just as a simplified evolutionary work would make generalized points about their supposed geological eras. Evolutionary "scientific" literature contains many more detailed analyses of a more specific nature, and, in an analogous manner, peer-reviewed creationist literature contains far more sophisticated analyses of these various ecosystems. Skeptics should not assume, therefore, that my simplifications are the last word on these ecosystems. Our model, in which we assume that sedimentary stratification reveals information about different geographical distributions of flora and fauna in the pre-Flood world, can be used in much greater depth than I intend to do here, and I recommend reading peer-reviewed journals, such as the *Answers Research Journal*, the *Journal of Creation*, or the *Creation Research Society Quarterly*, to name just three. As mentioned elsewhere, much of the background to my information comes from the work of Dr. Andrew Snelling in his indispensable *Earth's Catastrophic Past.*[19]

With this biblical presupposition, we can suppose that the pre-Flood world contained a number of large, generalized ecosystems, which are known as *biomes*. We suggest that there was a dinosaur-gymnosperm biome, as well as a mammalian-angiosperm-human biome. Other biomes that we might suggest include a hydrothermal-stromatolite biome and a lycopod-amphibian biome. I must repeat that there were likely to have been more than just these four biomes, and even these would have presented far more variation than this chapter can accommodate, but the descriptions below will help us to understand a great deal about the pre-Flood world.

Gymnosperms generally require warmer and more humid conditions than angiosperms. Therefore, it is suggested that the dinosaur-gymnosperm biomes would be located at low altitudes, probably near to the shores of the pre-Flood continent. The mammalian-angiosperm biomes would, therefore, be at higher altitudes. Snelling explains it thus:

> This is consistent with the description in Genesis of the river out of the Garden of Eden dividing into four rivers, which implies that the Garden of Eden, with its fruit trees and other angiosperms, mammals and man, was at a high point geographically.[20]

---

19. Andrew A. Snelling, *Earth's Catastrophic Past* (Dallas, TX: Institute for Creation Research, 2009), p. 727–737.
20. Ibid., p. 730.

If you refer to the chapter on the Flood's mechanism, you will see that the Catastrophic Plate Tectonics (CPT) model, which most modern creationists favor, suggests that the runaway subduction of the pre-Flood ocean basin was the engine that drove the Flood. Such an event would initially cause disruption of hydrothermal springs, and would take sediment from the ocean floor toward the land. Thus, the so-called "simple" stromatolite organisms would be the first biomes to be buried, and would therefore appear at the lower points of the Flood strata. Greater disturbance on the rising waters would disrupt the lycopods-amphibian biomes, because we propose that these biomes would probably comprise enormous floating forests. The reason why we think that there would be these unusual floating forest ecosystems will be explained later. Much of the material from these floating forests would sink and would provide the raw material for carboniferous coal deposits.

Eventually, the waters would rise onto the pre-Flood continent. The first biomes to be destroyed and buried would be the lower-altitude dinosaur-gymnosperm biomes, followed by the higher mammalian-angiosperm-human biomes. This geographical distribution of biomes neatly explains the general rules about why certain fossils are not usually found together, but also provides an easy way to explain the exceptional positioning of certain "out-of-place" fossils, which cannot be explained by the evolutionary, long-age model. For example, if someone did find a rabbit fossil in the Jurassic, then this Flood fossilization model would have no difficulty explaining it, as it would merely suppose that a rabbit was caught wandering outside its normal habitat.

Other effects of the rising floodwaters would serve to enhance the sorting effect caused by pre-Flood geographical distribution. Snelling mentions two such effects. The first is hydrodynamic selectivity. This simply uses the fact that particles of differing densities and shapes would have been moved by different amounts in the rising waters. This effect would cause more streamlined shapes, such as brachiopods, to be transported less far and therefore to form the lower strata. A second sorting effect would be that of greater mobility of land vertebrates. This helps explain why the lower strata would contain far more marine invertebrates than it would fish, which would have greater mobility. On land, it is likely that different animals would react to the rising waters in different ways — just as they do to stressful situations today. Some animals, therefore, would tend to stay in their habitats, while others would make a vain attempt to escape. These latter animals would be more likely to be found in higher strata.

It is worth mentioning that these latter two sorting effects would have a similar outcome to that produced by the geographical distribution model. It is likely that all three effects played their part in sorting the animals out, as some of them became trapped in sediment and fossilized.

Pre-Flood Floating Forests

One of the most unusual proposals for pre-Flood biomes is the suggestion that there may have been giant floating forests on the antediluvian ocean. The reason for this imaginative suggestion is found by looking at some of the fossils of giant lycopods. Dr. Kurt Wise, who proposed these floating forests, has given us a fascinating insight into his thought processes in developing this wonderful hypothesis.

Wise was trying to understand why a number of fossil plants were found with marine sediments and animals. His thoughts were taken back to his childhood, when he remembered being led on a field trip to a quaking bog. It occurred to him that the ecosystem best suggested by the combination of flora and fauna that he was studying would be something similar to a quaking bog. It was at this point that he came up with the idea of a vast floating forest.[21]

Coal beds in North America and Europe often occur with polystrate fossils of giant lycopods, some of which grew up to 150 feet (45 m).[22] Many of these fossils appear to have been hollow trunks, of the sort that could have grown as part of a large floating mat. The coal itself often seems to be formed from intertwined lycopod roots.

Wise has suggested that these plants could have formed the structure of giant floating islands. These floating forests would have developed soil around the lycopod roots. The whole forest would have been home to the unusual animals, such as unique amphibians, whose fossils have been found along with the lycopods. This whole biome would have been a unique environment. Once broken up by the rising floodwaters and the violent actions accompanying this process, the floating forest ecosystem would have been gone forever, reconstructed only in the imaginative and scientifically astute minds of creationists like Dr. Wise.

A Spiritual Lesson from Fossils

Everybody loves fossils. It is fun to find them in the rocks, and even more fun to chip them away from the rock matrix that contains them, so that you can take them home. To an evolutionist, they are simply a record of

---

21. Kurt Wise, "Sinking a Floating Forest," *Answers Magazine* (Oct–Dec 2008): p. 40–43.
22. Snelling, *Earth's Catastrophic Past*, p. 557.

a mythological past. But to the creationist, who trusts what God has said in His Word, they take on greater significance.

As Joshua led the Children of Israel across the Jordan into the Promised Land, they made a simple memorial by the side of the river. Each tribe contributed a stone — and I have always assumed that these were large stones, piled up on top of each other. Joshua explained to the people why he had made them do this.

> Joshua said to them: "Cross over before the ark of the LORD your God into the midst of the Jordan, and each one of you take up a stone on his shoulder, according to the number of the tribes of the children of Israel, that this may be a sign among you when your children ask in time to come, saying, 'What do these stones mean to you?' Then you shall answer them that the waters of the Jordan were cut off before the ark of the covenant of the LORD; when it crossed over the Jordan, the waters of the Jordan were cut off. And these stones shall be for a memorial to the children of Israel forever" (Joshua 4:5–7).

The stones were there so that the people could teach their children about what God had done.

Suppose your child shows you a fossil. He might ask, "What does this fossil mean?" How lame it would be to tell him the fairy story that is evolution. Instead, you can point out to him that the fossil is the remains, or the cast, of a dead creature. It died because God punished the people before the Flood because of their wickedness. It died because God brought an end to that first world. But in the midst of that Flood, He saved a remnant for Himself. He saved a man, who found grace in the eyes of the Lord, and his family.

In short, fossils are gospel tracts from over 4,000 years ago. You can tell your children about the judgment and salvation of God about His wrath and His mercy. That is what the fossils mean to us.

Chapter 11

The Design of the Ark

The word "ark" does not appear very often in the Hebrew text outside of Genesis. The word occurs 26 times in the four chapters from Genesis 6 through 9. The Hebrew word is *têbâh* (הבת), and can be found in Strong's concordances as H8392. It occurs again in Exodus 2:3 and Exodus 2:5.

> But when she could no longer hide him, she took an ark of bulrushes for him, daubed it with asphalt and pitch, put the child in it, and laid it in the reeds by the river's bank. And his sister stood afar off, to know what would be done to him. Then the daughter of Pharaoh came down to bathe at the river. And her maidens walked along the riverside; and when she saw the ark among the reeds, she sent her maid to get it (Exodus 2:3–5).

Most English versions refer to the vessel that carried Moses as a "basket." It would appear that a *têbâh* is some sort of closing box with a lid.

Later in the Bible, when we read about the ark of the covenant, the word *ark* is representing a different Hebrew word. So the only places where *têbâh* is mentioned are the 25 occasions in Genesis 6–9 and the two mentions in Exodus 2.

Scriptural Information on Design

The ark is one of the objects in the Bible that has a fairly detailed set of design instructions for it. A number of details are given that would enable good construction. However, there is also quite a lot left out of the biblical account, which leaves us to wonder how the ark might have been constructed and exactly what its shape was.

These are the things that we know for sure from Scripture about the design of the ark, with minimal conjecture about what each element means:

> Make yourself an ark of gopherwood; make rooms in the ark, and cover it inside and outside with pitch. And this is how you shall make it: The length of the ark shall be three hundred cubits, its width fifty cubits, and its height thirty cubits. You shall make a window for the ark, and you shall finish it to a cubit from above; and set the door of the ark in its side. You shall make it with lower, second, and third decks (Genesis 6:14–16).

God did not tell Noah to make a boat or a ship. The fact that early post-Flood civilizations soon had ships suggests that the pre-Flood civilization knew about boats and ships. But the *ark* was not going to be designed for motion or travel. It was to be designed to keep its occupants — humans and animals — safe. For that reason, God told Noah to make a *têbâh* — a container that would float and be stable and secure but without needing to navigate.

Gopherwood

The ark was to be made of *gopherwood*. Gopher is simply a transliteration from the Hebrew *gopher* (רפג), because we do not know what gopher actually was. The root of the word seems to suggest building, so gopher may have been a hardwood that was used for pre-Flood building. Our chapter on fossils shows us that there were many biomes or ecosystems before the Flood that no longer exist. This wood could be from one such type of tree. Perhaps, however, we could get some ideas from hardwoods of today that are used for some constructions.

There is a whole class of woods that are not actually related to each other, called ironwoods. One of these, which is native to Florida, is *Krugiodendron ferreum*, commonly known as *black ironwood*, or even *leadwood*. The special thing about these ironwoods is that they will sink in water, unlike most woods.

Water has a specific density of 1 $kgdm^{-3}$ (kilograms per cubic decimeter). Most woods have a specific density of less than this. For example, Scots Pine has a density of 0.51 $kgdm^{-3}$. Leadwood, however, has a density of 1.3 $kgdm^{-3}$, which means that it will sink in water.

Such ironwoods might have been the sort of very hard construction-type wood that is represented by gopherwood. But why choose a building material more dense than water? Well, steel is denser than water, and that works pretty well as a ship-building material. There would be more than enough air in an ironwood vessel to keep it afloat. The main issue is whether such woods would have provided the strong construction material required for such a very large vessel.

Rooms in the Ark

Next, Noah was told to "make *rooms* in the ark." What sort of rooms? The Hebrew word is *qên* (קן). This word represents nests or animal compartments, rather than ship berths. It is a source of constant amazement to me how many people write emails to me, ridiculing the account of the Flood by telling me that the two lions would have eaten the antelopes! Surely even common sense would suggest that Noah would have been bright enough to keep them apart. But God told Noah to make these compartments for the animals. For small animals, they could easily have been stacked several high on one of the decks, showing that there was more than enough room for all the animals on board.

Pitch

It is interesting that Noah was told to cover the vessel completely, inside and out, with *pitch*. The nature of this pitch has often been an interesting source of conjecture. It was obviously necessary to have pitch, because wood can often absorb water. The pitch must have been a waterproofing.

Today, the pitch that we would use would be bitumen. This is a heavy oil fraction, and is a by-product of refining petroleum oil. It has often been argued that the fossil fuels, like coal and oil, would have been formed in the Flood, because they would require the decomposition of dead organic material, and there is no obvious mechanism for the large-scale death of organisms before the Flood. There have been a number of articles in creationist literature about how oil might have formed during the Flood, but these are not necessary for this discussion, as the pitch was clearly applied before the Flood and it is unlikely that any fossil fuel would have been available before the Flood.

Perhaps the pre-Flood pitch was not bitumen. Dr. John Morris made these suggestions:

> This [pitch] may have been a resinous sap, the residue of heating wood without allowing it to burn, an animal-derived glue, or some

other concoction designed with the purpose of making the ark safe for its occupants. . . . Those on board the ark were, to a great degree, kept safe from the waters of the judgment by the action of the pitch.[1]

One interesting thing to note is that the Hebrew word that is translated here as pitch is *kâphar* (רפכ), which literally means covering. It is the same word used elsewhere in the Pentateuch to represent atonement.

> For the life of the flesh is in the blood, and I have given it to you upon the altar to make atonement for your souls; for it is the blood that makes atonement (*kâphar*) for the soul (Leviticus 17:11).

Noah and his family were protected against the watery judgment of God. We are protected against the fiery judgment of God to come, if we are under the covering of the atoning blood of Jesus Christ.

Window for the Ark

> You shall make a *window* for the ark, and you shall finish it to a cubit from above (Genesis 6:16, emphasis added).

The word used for window is puzzling. It is the Hebrew word *tsôhar* (רהצ) (Strong's number H6672). This is not the normal word for window, however. The usual word for window is *châllon* (ןולח) (H2474). For example:

> And it happened, as the ark of the covenant of the LORD came to the City of David, that Michal, Saul's daughter, looked through a *window* and saw King David whirling and playing music; and she despised him in her heart (1 Chronicles 15:29, emphasis added).

That is not to say that *tsôhar* is a rare word. It occurs 24 times in the Old Testament. But in every other occurrence, it is translated as "noon."

> And so it was, at *noon*, that Elijah mocked them and said, "Cry aloud, for he is a god; either he is meditating, or he is busy, or he is on a journey, or perhaps he is sleeping and must be awakened" (1 Kings 18:27, emphasis added).

Perhaps the word is referring to light. That is to say, the ark was to get its light from the "window" — hence, it might actually be a noon-light. However, even this does not fully help us identify it. The Old Testament, after all, uses another word for "light."

---

1. John D. Morris, *Pitch It!*, http://www.icr.org/article/pitch-it/, accessed 1/31/2012.

Then God said, "Let there be *light*"; and there was *light* (Genesis 1:3, emphasis added).

In Genesis 1:3, the word used for light is *ôr* (רוא) (H216). So the idea of *tsôphar* describing a light might perhaps be to do with its positioning — rather as we might say, in English, "the enemy soldiers are at 12 o'clock." Many creationists have, therefore, conjectured that the window or noon-light is some sort of long opening at the top of the roof of the ark. It is clear that such an opening would provide good ventilation for the ark — surely a necessary item on a vessel full of frightened, smelly animals!

One man who has done a great deal of research on the design of the ark is Tim Lovett. Anyone who wants to know more about basic ideas on the ark's design needs to consult his work. He has put together a beautiful coffee-table book,[2] and also maintains a highly detailed website.[3]

Lovett suggests that the noon-light window may have been a mechanism to allow ventilation, while keeping out water during the rolling motion of the vessel.

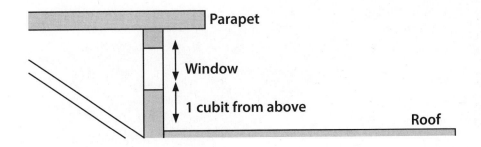

Lovett's thinking is as follows:

> "Finish it to a cubit from above" is closest to the Hebrew text, and seems to say that the window was finished to a cubit above the top. This would indicate a hatch combing, the usual way to prevent water from flowing into a hatch, and one cubit would be about the right height. By this reckoning, the window does not need to be restricted to a height of one cubit, although this would be adequate.[4]

2. Tim Lovett, *Noah's Ark: Thinking Outside the Box* (Green Forest, AR: Master Books, 2008).
3. www.worldwideflood.com, accessed 2/1/2012.
4. Lovett, *Noah's Ark: Thinking Outside the Box*, p. 25.

Door and Decks

The other two design elements mentioned (apart from dimensions, which I will discuss separately) are fairly easy to understand. The ark had a door and it had three decks. We can probably infer that there was only one door, and that this door could only be opened from the outside. The significance of this inference is discussed in the final chapter of the book. We can also probably infer that there would be some means of getting from deck to deck. For that reason, I really like Tim Lovett's picture of the ark design (below), where the biblical information is clearly labeled. But having been through the biblical information, we find that there are things that we are not told. We are not told, for example, what shape the ark is. Various ark researchers have differing opinions on this matter, and we will survey some of these, after a brief word about the dimensions of the ark.

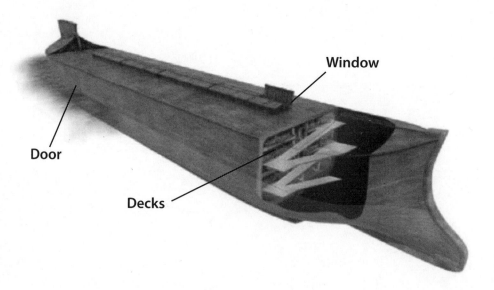

Dimensions and Technology

Erroneous presuppositions have been made in order to make negative comments about the ark. The principle criticism has been that it is supposed that people at the time of Noah would have been too primitive to build an ark of the size or sophistication being suggested here. However, the evidence suggests otherwise. Donald Chittick, for example, has presented a great deal of information about civilizations in the immediate post-Flood period, which leads us to suppose that they were using remembered pre-Flood technology.[5] Both John Woodmorappe[6] and Tim Lovett[7] have compiled much evidence to suggest that pre-Flood technology must have been at least as sophisticated as early Egyptian technology, and possibly more so.

Woodmorappe has carefully catalogued all the possible objections that he could think of as to why the ark could not have happened. He then shows that available technologies could easily have solved issues such as waste disposal and even automated feeding procedures, so that eight people could care for approximately 30,000 animals.

Lovett has done considerable research on early boat construction and has shown that technologies like mortise and tenon were available and used, and could explain how such a very large vessel could have been built using wood.

This moves us on to looking at the dimensions of the ark, both actual and relative. The ark was 300 cubits long, 50 cubits wide, and 30 cubits high. So, what is a cubit?

A cubit is the length of a man's forearm. Of course, this is not accurate enough for larger measurements, and many societies developed more standardized versions. For example, Egypt used a variety of cubits, such as the royal cubit, about 20.8 inches (529 mm).[8] Hebrew people used two main cubits. The long cubit was 20.4 inches (518 mm) and the short cubit was 17.5 inches (445 mm). It is more likely that the long cubit would have been used, making the ark about 510 feet (155 m) long, but most creationists tend to use the smaller number (giving a length of 438 feet, or 134 m) just to prove that the ark was feasible even in the "worst case" scenario.

The short cubit yields dimensions of 438 x 73 x 44 feet (134 x 22 x 13 m). This gives a capacity of 1.4 million cubic feet (or 40,000 m^3). The capacity of a standard North American railroad car for livestock is about 2,800 cubic feet.[9] Therefore, the ark had the capacity of about 495 railcars. Since each railcar can hold 240 sheep, the ark could accommodate over 118,000 sheep. One deck could accommodate 39,000 sheep.

Woodmorappe has estimated that there would have been about 8,000 kinds of land and flying animals before the Flood that needed to get on the

5. Donald F. Chittick, *The Puzzle of Ancient Man* (Newberg, OR: Creation Compass, 2006).
6. John Woodmorappe, *Noah's Ark: A Feasibility Study* (Dallas, TX: Institute for Creation Research, 1996).
7. Tim Lovett, *Noah's Ark: Impossible for Ancient People?* http://worldwideflood.com/objections/ancients_incapable.htm, accessed 2/1/2012.
8. http://en.wikipedia.org/wiki/Cubit, accessed 2/1/2012.
9. Information from U.S. Patent website.

ark. That would mean there would need to be 16,000 animals, the average size of which (including dinosaurs) is about that of a sheep. If Woodmorappe were half wrong, there would need to be 32,000 "sheep" on board, which would have fitted completely into one deck of the ark, if that is what was required. It can be seen, therefore, that the ark was more than large enough to carry all the animals, with perhaps a second deck used for food, leaving an entire animal-free deck for the eight people.

We have seen that the relative dimensions of the ark were 300 x 50 x 30. In a remarkable study carried out at the Korea Research Institute of Ships and Ocean Engineering (KRISO) in Daejeon, Korea, in 1992, nine staff research scientists, led by Dr. S.W Hong, carried out a study into the relative dimensions of ocean-going craft.[10] Their research showed that there were three considerations needed for safety on the ark. Maximum comfort would be achieved by maximizing the length, at the risk of the boat breaking in half. Maximum strength would occur if the height were increased, but this would destabilize the vessel. Maximum stability would be achieved by increasing the width, but this would make for a rough ride. The Korean study showed that the best compromise between these competing requirements was a set of relative dimensions of 300 x 50 x 30! What a remarkable coincidence!

Further Studies in Design

In the picture by Tim Lovett used earlier in this chapter, the reader would have seen an ark that looked somewhat different from the traditional box-shaped ark. The box-shaped ark is so often depicted that many have supposed it to be the actual biblical shape. One former colleague of mine once accused me of adding to Scripture by using Lovett's design. Yet Lovett's design has precisely the dimensions of the traditional box shape. Lovett has suggested that the ark may have had a tapered end to control the stability of movement, and a weather vane to catch the wind. He has based these thoughts on the shape of vessels from early post-Flood civilizations, such as the Sumerians. Other people who have produced excellent images and models of the ark include Johan Huibers[11] and Rod Walsh.[12]

---

10. S.W. Hong et al, "Safety Investigation of Noah's Ark in a Seaway," *Creation Ex Nihilo Technical Journal* 8(1) (1994): 26–35; http://creation.com/safety-investigation-of-noahs-ark-in-a-seaway, accessed 2/1/2012.

11. wikimedia.org/wikipedia/commons/8/8d/ArkVanJohan.jpg

12. http://www.answersingenesis.org.

Walsh's ark

Theological Significance

The ark is often said to be a *type* of Christ. This idea of *types* and *typology* can be a little confusing. It is a sort of living allegory. Thus, the ark was an actual, real vessel, but it also represents Jesus. Noah found grace in the eyes of the Lord, and was therefore saved from this watery judgment of God.

Huibers' ark

John Bunyan commented on Genesis 6:14 thus:

> The ark was a figure of several things. 1. Of Christ, in whom the church is preserved from the wrath of God. 2. It was a figure of the works of the faith of the godly: "By faith he prepared an ark"; by which the followers of Christ are preserved from the rage and tyranny of the world (for the rage of the water was a type of that, as I shall shew you hereafter). So then Noah, by preparing an ark, or by being bid so to do of God, was thereby admonished, first, to live by the faith of Christ, of whom the ark was a type: and hence it is said, that in preparing the ark, he "became heir of the righteousness which is by faith"; because he understood the mind of God therein, and throughout his figure acted faith upon Christ. But, Secondly, His faith was not to be idle, and therefore he was bid to work. This begat in him an obediential fear of doing ought which God had forbidden: "By faith Noah, being warned of God of things not seen as yet, moved with fear, prepared an ark, to the saving of his house; by the which he condemned the world, and became heir of the righteousness which is by faith" (Hebrews 11:7).[13]

---

13. John Bunyan, Paul F. Taylor, editor, *Genesis: A Commentary* (Leicester, J6D Publications, 2010), p. 178.

In his first epistle, Peter uses the ark as a type of Christ, as follows:

> For Christ also suffered once for sins, the just for the unjust, that He might bring us to God, being put to death in the flesh but made alive by the Spirit, by whom also He went and preached to the spirits in prison, who formerly were disobedient, when once the Divine longsuffering waited in the days of Noah, while the ark was being prepared, in which a few, that is, eight souls, were saved through water (1 Peter 3:18–20).

Peter directly compares the ark to Jesus. We can understand physically how the ark could save eight people from destruction. In the same way, therefore, Jesus saves those who repent and trust in Him from the judgment of God at the end of the age.

An interesting additional thought — one that I will develop in the final chapter of the book — is that the ark was covered, as we have seen, in pitch, which means atonement. Pitch waterproofed Noah's family against God's judgment. Jesus' atoning blood fireproofs us against the fiery judgment of God to come.

Summary and Conclusion

Generations of children have been shown childish pictures of Noah's ark that are impossible. The illustration below[14] was created by Answers in

Genesis in order to illustrate the sort of cute image that they, like me, don't like! Such images undermine respect for Scripture. Such an ark is clearly impossible, but if it is presented as an illustration to a Bible story, the impression is given that the whole Bible account is a fairy story, rather than historical fact.

The Bible's ark is very different. The dimensions of the ark are realistic. The descriptions of the parts of the ark that we know about make sense. It is soberly described, in a down-to-earth manner. It was the means of salvation for Noah and his family and is a type of Christ, explaining how Jesus saves us from the wrath to come.

---

14. http://www.answersingenesis.org/assets/images/articles/2006/07/ark-1.jpg.

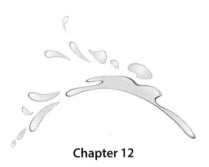

Chapter 12

The Animals Came in Two by Two

I t is often a source of amazement to me how many things are difficult for unbelievers to understand. Accusations against various parts of the Flood account are frequently made, such as: "This is impossible, so obviously the Flood did not happen." The questioners — who usually do not actually want an answer — are often not aware that their questions are full of pre-suppositions.

An example of such a question is this: "How did Noah catch all the animals that he needed to take in the ark?" Although we will answer this question below, it is better to first tackle the nature of skeptical questions. They are almost always presuppositional.

Farrell Till criticizes the Flood account thus:

> If Bible fundamentalists are honest, then, they will have to admit that the Genesis writer intended his story to be understood as an account of a flood that had covered the entire earth. In other words, he expected us to believe that within the space of forty days enough water rained down or rose from "the fountains of the deep" to cover the highest mountain on earth to a depth of 15 cubits (7:20). In prescientific times when people knew very little about geography and meteorology, a claim like this could find general acceptance, but in modern times only the very credulous can believe it.

To understand this, we have only to analyze the story in terms of the number of inches of rain per minute that would have had to fall on the entire surface of the earth to produce the results described in Genesis 7–8 . We now know, for example, that Mount Everest is the highest mountain "under the whole heaven." It reaches an altitude of 29,028 feet, which would be a height of 348,336 inches. For enough rain to fall in a period of 40 days to reach the peak of this mountain, the cloud formations would have to drop 8,708 inches of rain per day uniformly over all the earth. This would amount to 363 inches per hour or six inches per minute. Can any reasonable person believe that it once rained continuously for 40 days and nights at an average rate of six inches per minute? A rainfall of six inches in one day is a veritable downpour. What would six inches per minute sustained for 57,600 continuous minutes be like?[1]

Till's skepticism is based on presupposition. He has assumed that the topography of the pre-Flood world would be the same as today — in other words, that high mountains like Mount Everest existed before the Flood. That would not make sense. He also assumes that the rain was the main source of water for the Flood. Even though he has read about the "fountains of the deep," he has not noticed that, being listed first, they would constitute the greater source of flood water.

Similar objections can be made to the questioning of how the animals were "captured." In this chapter, we will look at these sort of scornful questions and suggest how the animals got to the ark, as well as how they scattered over the world after the Flood.

How Did the Animals Get to the Ark?

The skeptics who ask questions like the one above clearly have not done their homework. The Bible says nothing about Noah having to catch animals to put them on the ark. This would have been an impossible task, but it would not, in any case, have been necessary. The Bible makes it clear that Noah did not have to go and find the animals.

> Of the birds after their kind, of animals after their kind, and of every creeping thing of the earth after its kind, two of every kind will come to you to keep them alive (Genesis 6:20).

1. Farrell Till, *Common Sense and Noah's Flood*, http://www.infidels.org/library/magazines/tsr/1993/2/2noah93.html, 1933, accessed 2/6/2012.

Obviously, skeptics have a problem with the idea that the animals just came to Noah. However, the whole of this account is about supernatural happenings that do not just take place by themselves. Therefore, it was God who decided that the animals should go to Noah and made it happen.

God could have made the animals go to Noah by any means He chose. However, there are some interesting natural migration behaviors that God might have used.

Many animals have a migration pattern so that they can move to areas of more conducive climates at different times of the year. One of the most remarkable of these is that of the monarch butterfly. Its unusual migration is described thus on the CreationWiki website:

> The Monarch butterfly is a long-distance migrator. They begin massive southward migrations in August until the first frost. The northward migration begins in the spring. However, individual butterflies don't complete the migration both ways. Their great-grandchildren end up back at the starting point. In North America there are two large population groups that follow different migration paths. Most Monarchs east of the Rocky Mountains overwinter in the Sierra Madres in central Mexico where they live in fir forests at high altitudes. Far western groups of monarchs winter along the coast of southern California, where they live in groves of pine, cypress, and eucalyptus trees. In the spring they head north and breed along the way. The original butterfly dies along the way, but the offspring it leaves behind continues north, where the cycle will start again in the fall.[2]

How does a monarch butterfly know to make its way to a place that neither it nor its parents have ever been? What sort of programming do these amazing insects contain? Whatever the case may be, there is something inside each insect that obliges it to make this strange multi-generational migration. Could God have used a similar means to bring animals to Noah?

Another possible animal instinct is that of the homing pigeon. One experimenter has summarized this ability, in the abstract to his scientific article.

> Homing pigeons can return from distant, unfamiliar release points. Experienced pigeons can do so even if they are transported,

2. "Monarch Butterfly," CreationWiki, http://creationwiki.org/Monarch_butterfly, accessed 2/7/2012.

anesthetized, and deprived of outward journey information. Airplane tracking has shown that they make relatively straight tracks on their homeward journey; therefore, pigeons must have some way of determining the home direction at the release site.[3]

This unusual ability that pigeons have could also be something that God used to send the animals to Noah. In practice, I think it is more likely that the event was simply a miraculous event and that we probably need to look no further for a naturalistic explanation than we would look for one to explain how Jesus could walk on water. Jesus could defy gravity and walk on water because He created the water and the gravity.

One factor that would facilitate the migration of animal pairs to the ark is the fact that the pre-Flood world probably consisted of one super-continent, or *Pangaea*. Therefore, there would be no oceanic barrier to the animals reaching the ark. Of course, the post-Flood world would be different, comprised as it is of the continents that we have today. The recolonization of the world by post-Flood migration will be discussed later.

Noah Couldn't Fit Two of Every Species on the Ark

This objection is entirely correct. There is no way that Noah could fit two of every species onto the ark. There could be about 100 million species of animals. This would require 200 million animals or so. There wouldn't be room on the ark.

Once more, the objection is caused by a presuppositional error. The skeptic has supposed that the term *kind* in the Bible (Hebrew *mîn* מין) is the same as the scientific term *species*. This is not the case. Creation biologists use the word *baramin* ("created kind") to identify this classification. There isn't a direct correlation between evolutionary and biblical taxonomy. However, the *baramin* is closer to the evolutionary *family*, rather than species.

It is observable that new species develop within a baramin, because there is an existing gene pool from which there can be selection. For example, since tigers and lions can hybridize, they must be in the same baramin. Therefore, Noah did not take two lions and two tigers on the ark — he simply took two of the cat baramin, from which the current species have developed since the Flood. With this definition of baramins or kinds, we see that a lot fewer animals were needed on the ark.

---

3. Charles Walcott, "Pigeon Homing: Observations, Experiments and Confusions," *The Journal of Experimental Biology* 199, 21–27 (1996); http://jeb.biologists.org/content/199/1/21.full.pdf, accessed 2/7/2012.

Now let's see exactly what sorts of animals were needed on the ark.

> On the very same day Noah and Noah's sons, Shem, Ham, and Japheth, and Noah's wife and the three wives of his sons with them, entered the ark — they and every beast after its kind, all cattle after their kind, every creeping thing that creeps on the earth after its kind, and every bird after its kind, every bird of every sort. And they went into the ark to Noah, two by two, of all flesh *in which is the breath of life* (Genesis 7:13–15, emphasis added).

These verses restrict what sort of animals were required on the ark. It makes sense that no fish or marine creatures were needed, as they would be able to survive. What is not quite so obvious is that invertebrates were not required on the ark either. The animals on the ark were likely to be land vertebrates, because Genesis 7:15 says that they were to be animals "in which is the breath of life," which implies that they would have lungs. The three groups of land animals, as defined by the Bible, were to be represented — the beasts, the cattle, and the creeping things. I wrote elsewhere, commenting on day 6 of the creation week, about these three classifications:

> It would appear that the three classifications of land animals have nothing to do with taxonomic classification. Instead, it is a fairly practical and pragmatic classification, relating to how these animals were to interact with mankind. . . . "Beasts of the earth" probably refers to large wild animals. "Cattle" suggests domesticated animals. The "creeping things" are those lower to the ground, and therefore of less immediate importance to mankind.[4]

The "creeping things" in Genesis 1:24 probably include invertebrates, such as insects, which fact explains why they are specifically excluded here. Insects and other invertebrates would have survived Flood conditions, as they do today, by means such as dormancy, laying eggs, and clinging to rafts of uprooted vegetation. John Woodmorappe has written at length on this subject.[5]

It should also be noted that a fourth group of animals is included. These are the birds, or, as the KJV puts it, fowl. In my book *The Six Days of Genesis*, I explained how the Hebrew word *ôph* is a much wider term than birds,

---

4. Paul F. Taylor, *The Six Days of Genesis* (Green Forest, AR: Master Books, 2007), p. 70.
5. John Woodmorappe, *Noah's Ark: A Feasibility Study* (Dallas, TX: Institute for Creation Research, 2003).

and refers to flying creatures in general, including bats and, probably, ptero-dactyls. The Bible includes flying insects under the heading of *ôph*,[6] again underlining why creatures without lungs did not need to be on the ark. The fact that God required flying creatures on the ark is strong evidence that the Flood was global and not local. If the Flood were merely a local event, why would birds be required on the ark, when they could easily have flown away, beyond the edge of the Flood?

If you read the chapter on the ark, you will also see that it is very easy to explain how there could be sufficient room on board the ark for all the animals required. In short, Woodmorappe has suggested about 16,000 baramins, hence just over 32,000 animals (there were seven pairs of every clean animal). The average size of these animals would be that of a sheep. Therefore, the ark needed enough capacity to house 32,000 sheep. Just one deck out of the three available would have been more than sufficient to accommodate this quantity of livestock.

Recolonizing the World

After the Flood, the animals would need to spread out over the surface of the planet again. This migration would have to have been relatively rapid, and our model for understanding this needs to take into account the changed environments and topography of the world. In developing a biblical model for this recolonization, we need to consider the following.

- As stated above, it was pairs of the biblical *kinds* or baramins that got off the ark and recolonized the world, becoming more diverse within their kinds with each successive generation.

- We also stated above that God brought the animals to Noah. Because of this fact, we can infer that it was God's will for each of these baramins to survive, at least initially, after the Flood. Therefore, the recolonization of the land masses was determined by God. It was not left to chance.

- The ark came to rest in the region known as Ararat (Genesis 8:4). This may not have been exactly on modern Mount Ararat. Indeed, it is unlikely that the ark could have come to rest on the peak of a mountain. However, the landing would have been among the mountainous areas of what is now eastern Turkey, perhaps as far as western Iran.

---

6. In Leviticus 11:23, the Hebrew *ôph* has been translated as "flying" in the KJV and NKJV, but is the same word that was translated as *bird* or *fowl* in Leviticus 11:13

- God decided that the earth would be recolonized. The abundance and multiplication of the animals was also God's will.

> Then God spoke to Noah, saying, "Go out of the ark, you and your wife, and your sons and your sons' wives with you. Bring out with you every living thing of all flesh that is with you: birds and cattle and every creeping thing that creeps on the earth, so that they may abound on the earth, and be fruitful and multiply on the earth." So Noah went out, and his sons and his wife and his sons' wives with him. Every animal, every creeping thing, every bird, and whatever creeps on the earth, according to their families, went out of the ark (Genesis 8:15–19).

The recolonization model that I suggest in this chapter attempts to remain faithful to the above principles. Remember that the Bible is inspired, but our scientific models are not. If I subsequently find this model to be untenable, this would not shake my commitment to the absolute authority of Scripture.

One accusation that is frequently thrown at biblical creationists is that kangaroos could not have hopped to Australia, because there are no fossils of kangaroos en route. But the expectation of such fossilization is a presuppositional error. Such an expectation happens because of the assumption that fossils take time to form and that such fossils are inevitable from animal populations. That this view is mistaken is easily shown. Consider the hundreds of thousands of bison that used to roam the plains and prairies of North America. Despite these huge numbers, hardly any bison fossils are found there. Similarly, we know that there were lions in Israel in Bible times, but no fossils of lions have been found there. Fossilization is by no means inevitable. It usually requires sudden, rapid burial. Otherwise, the bones would decompose before permineralization was possible.

It is useful to compare this situation with modern recolonizations. For example, the *Encyclopædia Britannica* has the following to say about Surtsey Island and Krakatoa and the multiplication of species.

> Six months after the eruption of a volcano on the island of Surtsey off the coast of Iceland in 1963, the island had been colonized by a few bacteria, molds, insects, and birds. Within about a year of the eruption of a volcano on the island of Krakatoa in the tropical Pacific in 1883, a few grass species, insects, and vertebrates had taken

hold. On both Surtsey and Krakatoa, only a few decades had elapsed before hundreds of species reached the islands. Not all species are able to take hold and become permanently established, but eventually the island communities stabilize into a dynamic equilibrium.[7]

Non-flying animals could easily have traveled from the Ararat region to the outer parts of the world after the Flood. They could have made the journey by a variety of means. Some may have floated on logs and vegetation rafts, leftovers from the massive pre-Flood floating forests that were ripped up during the Flood and likely remained afloat for many decades on the world's new oceans, transported by currents. Others could later have been taken to places by people. For example, Savolainen has suggested that all Australian dingoes are descended from a single female domesticated dog from Southeast Asia.[8] Another possibility is that animals could have crossed land bridges. This is, after all, how both animals and people are presumed by evolutionists to have migrated from Asia to the Americas, by using a land bridge at the Bering Straits. For such land bridges to have existed, we must assume that sea levels were lower in the immediate post-Flood period than they are today. The best creationist explanation for how this may have occurred is probably the concept of a post-Flood Ice Age.

Ice Age

The idea of a post-Flood Ice Age has been discussed by the creationist researcher Michael Oard.[9] His theory is that an Ice Age may have followed closely after the Flood. Oard proposes that seismic activity during the Flood may have caused the Ice Age. The dust and aerosols in the atmosphere would have kept the atmosphere colder than it is today. At the same time, volcanic activity in the new oceans would have rendered the oceans warmer than today. Thus, the oceans would have evaporated more than at present, with the vapor hitting a cold atmosphere, causing solid precipitation as snow. Coincidentally, his ideas suggest that the sea itself would have been free from ice. Therefore, the Ice Age would have been a period when the Arctic Ocean was free of ice, and humans would have been able to migrate by the famed

---

7. Encyclopædia Britannica, http://www.britannica.com/EBchecked/topic/129392/community-ecology/70600/Community-equilibrium-and-species-diversity, accessed 2/7/2012.

8. Peter Savolainen et al., "A Detailed Picture of the Origin of the Australian Dingo, Obtained from the Study of Mitochondrial DNA," *PNAS* (Proceedings of the National Academy of Sciences of the United States of America) 101:12387–12390 (August 2004).

9. See, for example, Michael Oard, *An Ice Age Caused by the Genesis Flood* (Dallas, TX: Institute for Creation Research, 1990).

northwest and northeast passages. Oard's theory suggests an Ice Age lasting no more than 500 years.

The climatic changes associated with this Ice Age could have triggered the many extinctions that occurred. And the theory also gives a useful model to explain the existence of land bridges due to lower ocean levels.

Certain features from the Ice Age are shown by Oard to be problems for the evolutionist, but not for the creationist. For example, there is the fact of disharmonious association of fossils — fossils of creatures normally associated with different conditions (such as creatures with a preference for hot and cold climates) being found in close proximity. Oard's book mentions a couple of these — such as a fossilized hippopotamus found near a reindeer fossil.

Oard has suggested that even with present topography, a number of significant land bridges would have existed to facilitate migrations if the sea level were only 180 feet (55 m) below current levels. However, there is even evidence that the land in some places where land bridges would be necessary could have been higher still. The idea of land bridges is a useful model to explain how some migrations could have occurred.

There are still some skeptics, however, who doubt that there could have been land bridges all the way to Australia. There are rational explanations as to how animals may have reached the far corners of the world. Of course, we were not there at the time to witness this migration, but those who stick to a biblical worldview can be certain that animals did get to far places, and that there are reasonable theories about how it could have happened.

So we should have no problem accepting the Bible as true. Creationist scientific models of animal migration work better than those of the evolutionists. The reason such models are rejected is that they do not fit in with the orthodox, secular evolutionary worldview.

It is not a problem for us to rationalize why certain animals do not appear in certain parts of the world. Why, for example, does Australia have such unusual fauna, including so many marsupials? Marsupials are, of course, known elsewhere in the world. For example, opossums are found in North and South America, and fossilized marsupials have been found elsewhere. But in many places, climatic changes and other factors could lead to their extinction.

The lack of great marsupials in other continents need be no more of a problem than the lack of dinosaurs. As with many species today, they just died out — a reminder of a sin-cursed world. One proposed theory is that marsupials — because they bore their young in pouches — were able to travel farther and faster than mammals that had to stop to care for their young. They were able to establish themselves in far-flung Australia before competitors reached the continent.

Similar models could be built about the many unusual bird species in New Zealand, on islands from which mammals were absent until the arrival of European settlers.

Recolonization Theory

I need to say a word about the so-called recolonization theory. I have said a lot about recolonization, but the model known as the recolonization theory[10] is somewhat different. It is a theory developed by certain European creationists that suggests that the fossil record is actually a record, not of catastrophe, but of processes occurring during recolonization.

Proponents of this theory suggest that the Flood completely obliterated the earth's previous crust so that none of the present fossils were caused by it. To accommodate fossilization processes, recolonization theory suggests that the age of the earth be stretched by a few thousand years. Some advocates of this view suggest an age of about 8,000 years for the earth, while others suggest figures as high as 20,000 years.

A detailed criticism of recolonization theory has previously been published by McIntosh, Edmondson, and Taylor,[11] and another by Holt.[12]

The principal error of this view is that it starts from supposed scientific anomalies, such as the fossil record, rather than from Scripture. This has led to the proposals among some recolonizers, but not all, that there must be gaps in the genealogies recorded in Genesis 5 and 11, even though there is no need for such gaps. Indeed, the suggestion of gaps in these genealogies causes further doctrinal problems.[13]

Even the views of those recolonizers who do not expand the genealogies contain possible seeds of compromise. Because the recolonizers accept the

---

10. This is spelled *recolonisation* in the UK, which is where the theory began.
11. A.C. McIntosh, Tom Edmondson, and Steve Taylor, "Flood Models: The Need for an Integrated Approach," *TJ* 14(1) (April 2000): 52–59; A.C. McIntosh, Tom Edmondson, and Steve Taylor, "Genesis and Catastrophe," *TJ* 14(1) (April 2000): 101–109. Recolonizers' disagreements with these article were answered in A.C. McIntosh, Tom Edmondson, and Steve Taylor, "McIntosh, Taylor, and Edmondson reply to Flood Models," *TJ* 14(3) (2000): 80–82, available online at http://www.answersingenesis.org/articles/tj/v14/n3/flood-reply, accessed 2/7/2012.
12. R. Holt, "Evidence for a Late Cainozoic Flood/Post-Flood Boundary," *TJ* 10(1) (April 1996): 128–168.
13. Ken Ham and Larry Pierce, "Who Begat Whom?" *Answers Magazine* (1) 2, http://www.answersingenesis.org/articles/am/v1/n2/who-begat-whom, accessed 2/7/2012.

geologic column, and because the Middle East has a great deal of what is called Cretaceous rock, it follows that the Middle East would need to be submerged after the Flood, at the very time of the Tower of Babel events in Genesis 11. This has led some of the recolonizers to speculate that the ark actually landed in Africa and, therefore, that continent was the host to the events of Genesis 11 and 12. This would seem to be a very weak position exegetically and historically. Such exegetical weaknesses led Professor Andy McIntosh and his colleagues to comment, "Their science is driving their interpretation of Scripture, and not the other way round."[14]

Summary and Conclusions

We should not be surprised or downhearted at the accusations by skeptics with their criticism of the Bible. Many people will believe all sorts of odd things, whatever the logic, rather than believing the truth of God's Word.

Having started this model, as with all our models, with the presupposition that the Bible is true, we have seen that scientific models can be developed to explain how the animals migrated after the Flood. These models are consistent with observed data and the accounts given in the Bible. Interestingly, opponents of biblical creationism are prepared to use similar models in their evolutionary explanations of animal migrations. Of course, our model may be superseded one day. Even so, it is important to note that biblically consistent models exist and make sense. The fact of animal migration around the world is illustrative of the goodness and graciousness of God, who provided above and beyond our needs.[15]

14. Letter to the editor, *TJ* 14(3) (2000): 80–82.
15. Much of the material in this chapter is based on the author's earlier writing on the subject: Paul F. Taylor, "How Did Animals Spread All Over the World from Where the Ark Landed?" in Ken Ham, editor, *The New Answers Book 1* (Green Forest, AR: Master Books, 2006).

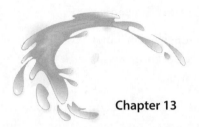

Chapter 13

Radiometric Dating and the Flood

What does a discussion about radiometric dating have to do with the Flood? In fact, it has a great deal of relevance. I can summarize many of the scientific arguments used about dating methods thus: radiometric dating methods, while accurate, are calculated using faulty assumptions. If the Flood is factored into the equation, then the discrepancies become immediately understandable.

Are Radiometric Dating Methods Inaccurate?

It is very important that creationists be respectful in their choice of language when applying their justified criticisms of scientific methods. It always looks bad when an amateur creationist speaker, who may well not have any science qualification from an accredited source, weighs in on the subject of radiometric dating with statements such as "Carbon dating is not accurate." Such arrogance is rightly condemned when you consider that such a critic of secular dating methods is attempting single-handedly to undermine the work of a PhD physicist. Please do not misunderstand what I am saying. There are clear problems with radiometric dating, most of which are easily understandable by people who do not have a degree in physics. Nevertheless, it is nonsense to accuse qualified scientific minds of inaccuracy, when their lives and career depend on their care and expertise in experimental science. I need to underline this point: radiometric dating is NOT inaccurate.

It is carried out by people who know what they are doing. It is carried out with very high levels of accuracy and scientific integrity.

The problem is not, in fact, the experimental accuracy. The problem with radiometric dating is the presupposition on which the calculations of radiometric age are made. The principal presupposition of any radiometric dating method is *uniformitarianism*.

Uniformitarianism

This big word, which would give you a high score in Scrabble™, should be the correct basis for our criticism of radiometric dating. Our criticism begins, as it should, with Scripture.

> Knowing this first: that scoffers will come in the last days, walking according to their own lusts, and saying, "Where is the promise of His coming? For since the fathers fell asleep, all things continue as they were from the beginning of creation." For this they willfully forget: that by the word of God the heavens were of old, and the earth standing out of water and in the water, by which the world that then existed perished, being flooded with water (2 Peter 3:3–6).

The scoffers are those who refuse to believe what God says in His Word. The reason they refuse to believe what God says in His Word is that they are "walking according to their own lusts." This is a topic for another chapter! However, we can analyze the substance of their scoffing. They despise the whole of Scripture, including what the Bible has to say about Jesus. Have you ever heard people accuse you, saying things like, "If God is a God of love, why does He allow suffering in the world? Why doesn't He come back and sort everything out?" Such people are committed to a naturalistic interpretation of the world. They do not expect God to do something, because they don't believe in Him, so they say — yet they still blame Him for everything that has gone wrong! Talk about wanting to have your cake and eat it!

This is the substance of the scoffers' accusation: "Where is the promise of His coming? For since the fathers fell asleep, all things continue as they were from the beginning of creation." The accusation is in the words "Where is the promise of His coming?" The reason for their scoffing is "For since the fathers fell asleep, all things continue as they were from the beginning of creation." We need to look at their reason for scoffing in more detail. Do these people believe in Genesis and creation? No, they do not.

The phrase "beginning of creation" is a specific Greek phrase, which refers to the beginning of everything. In modern secular terms, such people could be referring to the big bang, or some other beginning event. It is then their contention that "all things continue as they were from the beginning of creation." In other words, any naturalistic process that they observe can have its rate of change measured, and it is their assumption that such rates of change have never, ever changed since the beginning, or since the big bang. They are referring to a universe without God, where processes are slow and unchanging and leave no possibility for the miraculous intervention of God. Modern evolutionary thinking and dating is entirely based on the idea that rates of physical processes have not changed. This principle is known as uniformitarianism, and it is both unbiblical and unscientific, as we shall observe.

The reason why uniformitarianism is unbiblical is because the scoffers have left two important events out of the equation. These two events are the creation and the Flood.

> By the word of God the heavens were of old, and the earth standing out of water and in the water, by which the world that then existed perished, being flooded with water (2 Peter 3:5–6).

These two events are "by the word of God," a phrase with two implications. One implication is that it is the Bible that provides us with the information on these events. We are therefore being reminded that we are not to interpret the Bible by events, but rather interpret events by the Bible. Peter is hammering home the point that the Bible is true, and is to be our paradigm for the way we interpret everything. The second implication is that these events happened because of the direct intervention and action of God. Therefore, a philosophy like the one the scoffers have, which supposedly eliminates the need for God, is self-defeating and to be dismissed as nonsense.

Of course, these scoffers should know this: Romans 1 should always be in our minds as we try to understand the reason for scoffing and failure to believe God.

> For the wrath of God is revealed from heaven against all ungodliness and unrighteousness of men, who suppress the truth in unrighteousness, because what may be known of God is manifest in them, for God has shown it to them. For since the creation of the world His

invisible attributes are clearly seen, being understood by the things that are made, even His eternal power and Godhead, so that they are without excuse, because, although they knew God, they did not glorify Him as God, nor were thankful, but became futile in their thoughts, and their foolish hearts were darkened (Romans 1:18–21).

That is why Peter describes such people as being "willfully ignorant." My colleague, Eric Hovind, describes this amusingly as being "stupid on purpose." The NIV translates this phrase as "they deliberately forget." They refuse to accept the reality of God's miraculous power, even though His power is obvious and self-evident. They would, however, prefer to return to a uniformitarian myth that everything has always proceeded in this way, and they metaphorically stick their fingers in their ears and sing "la la la!" very loudly, if we try to explain the truth to them. Their position is not logical or scientific. The problem is that their entire thinking is based on the wrong presuppositions. Uniformitarianism is a presuppositional position. The correct presuppositional position is that God is in control, He is the Creator, and He judges sin. This correct presupposition makes much more sense of the scientific data on the subject of dating methodology.

Carbon Dating

Carbon dating is misunderstood and misapplied by evolutionists and creationists alike. In my criticism of evolutionists, I am not, at the moment, criticizing evolutionary scientists, who know the limitations of carbon dating. I am criticizing the ordinary person who believes in evolution, especially newspaper journalists and television presenters, many of whom do not understand the science that they are writing or talking about.

Hardly a week goes by that I don't receive an email along these lines: "Some dinosaur fossils have been found and they have been carbon-dated to be 100 million years old." Comments such as these display an ignorance of carbon dating. Such a statement must be untrue, for two reasons: (1) Carbon dating cannot yield dates older than 100,000 years old, and (2) the fossil would not normally be expected to have any of the original organic carbon present, because a fossilized bone is a mineralized impression of a bone in the rock, rather than being the actual original bone.

Before I go on to justify these two points, I should also point out that many creationists are ignorant of carbon dating when they oppose it with puerile statements such as "carbon dating is inaccurate" or "carbon dating is unreliable."

Many elements with more than one isotope exist. The chemical properties of an element are mostly governed by its atomic number, which is the
number of protons in the nucleus of the atom. (This number also determines the number of electrons, and, by simple chemical rules, the numbers of electrons in each atomic orbital, thereby determining the chemistry
of the element, which is largely concerned with the transfer or sharing of
electron density from the orbitals). It is possible to have atoms with different numbers of neutrons in the nucleus, but the same number of protons.
These atoms will behave in a similar manner chemically, because they have
the same atomic number. Because the atomic number of each element is
unique, the atomic number determines what element an atom actually is.

Carbon has an atomic number of 6. Therefore, all carbon atoms, by
definition, will have 6 protons in them. However, some carbon atoms have
6 neutrons, some have 7, and some have 8. As the mass of the atoms is
found by adding the number of protons and neutrons, which are nearly the
same mass, we can have carbon atoms with masses of 12, 13, and 14. These
atoms would be labeled as ^{12}C, ^{13}C, and ^{14}C, often written, for convenience,
as carbon-12 etc. or C-12 etc. C-14 has an unstable nucleus and decays by
emitting a β-particle, to form nitrogen-14.

$$^{14}_{6}C \rightarrow ^{14}_{7}N + ^{0}_{-1}\beta$$

This decay event is a random event. Although one cannot say anything
about the nature of an individual radioactive decay event, we can make
predictions about large numbers of such events. After a given time (known
as the half-life, or $t_{1/2}$), half of the C-14 atoms will have decayed into stable
N-14 (nitrogen) atoms. After another $t_{1/2}$ period, half of the remainder will
have decayed, leaving a quarter of the original C-14 atoms. This half-life can
be calculated from the observed rate of decay. The normal half-life for C-14
is 5,730 years.

Chemically, C-14 will behave like every other atom of carbon. Com-
pounds in living organisms contain carbon atoms. Therefore, some of these
carbon atoms will be C-14 atoms. A living organism is assumed to have an
equilibrium of C-14 atoms, because, as the atoms decay, they are replaced by
fresh C-14 atoms, from food, for example. So, while the organism is alive,
the proportion of C-14 should remain constant. After it has died, however,
there will only be decay of C-14, without replacement by food. If the half-life
of C-14 has remained constant, then we can use its measurement to calculate

how long ago the specimen died, but only if we can make some assumptions: how much C-14 was in the organism when it died, that the half-life never changed during the lifetime of the organism or after its subsequent death, and that no C-14 has been gained or lost by the main operating scientist. We will examine these assumptions in the section on uranium dating. For now,

Diamond

if we pretend that these unreasonable assumptions are true, it still leaves us with a dilemma. After 10 half-lives (57,300 years), there should not be an appreciable amount of C-14 left. Yet C-14 tests on diamonds — some supposedly billions of years old, based on the rock layers they are found in — often reveal positive results, which would be impossible if the diamonds were more than about 60,000 years old. Please do not misunderstand the point that I am making. I do not accept that such diamonds actually are 60,000 years old, because the Bible teaches that the earth is about 6,000 years old. But the figure of 60,000 is mentioned to show that a uranium date of several million years on the same sample would be impossible.

The quantity of C-14 in the atmosphere (existing in molecules of CO_2) remains constant, because of its rate of formation from N-14 atoms in the atmosphere, by bombardment of the earth's atmosphere by neutrinos. However, if the rate of bombardment had ever been different in the past, then we would not be able to assume a constant quantity of C-14. Even old-age secular scientists now do not believe that the rate of bombardment by solar neutrinos has always been constant, so the reliability of C-14 dates is called into question. However, the reliability of C-14 is not as great an issue as the fact that it simply does not yield the ages of millions of years that popular commentators (but not serious evolutionists) suggest for it.

Uranium-Lead Dating

Uranium-lead dating (abbreviated using the chemical symbols to U-Pb) relies on measurement of a similar radioactive process, albeit with a much longer half-life. This is the decay series of the radioactive but naturally occurring isotope U-238 to stable Pb-206.

$$^{238}_{92}U \rightarrow \alpha + {}^{234}_{90}Th \rightarrow \beta + {}^{234}_{91}Pa \rightarrow \beta + {}^{234}_{92}U \rightarrow \alpha + {}^{230}_{90}Th \rightarrow \alpha + {}^{226}_{88}Ra \rightarrow \alpha + {}^{222}_{86}Rn \rightarrow \alpha + {}^{218}_{84}Po$$
$$\rightarrow \beta + {}^{218}_{85}At \rightarrow \beta + {}^{218}_{86}Rn \rightarrow \alpha + {}^{214}_{84}Po \rightarrow \alpha + {}^{210}_{82}Pb \rightarrow \beta + {}^{210}_{83}Bi \rightarrow \beta + {}^{210}_{84}Po$$
$$\rightarrow \alpha + {}^{206}_{82}Pb$$

Those who have studied some basic chemistry will understand the numbers. Those who have not can at least see the following: for one atom of U-238 to decay to Pb-206, there will be 8 α-particles and 6 β-particles emitted. An α (alpha) particle is really a helium nucleus. The α-particle could obtain 2 electrons and become an He (helium) atom.

The half-life of U-238 is 4.47 billion years. Do I believe this? Yes, I do! You have to understand what half-life means. It does not have anything to do with how long the uranium has been around. It is merely the theoretical length of time that the uranium would need to be around for half of its atoms to have decayed into lead-206. So it is completely possible for me to accept that U-238 has a $t_{1/2}$ of 4.47 billion years, even though the earth is only 6,000 years old. It just means that not a lot of the uranium has decayed yet, though the amount that has decayed is measurable.

A group of creation scientists began a research project in 1997, called Radioisotopes and the Age of the Earth, or RATE.[1] This important project commissioned a number of experiments and produced a series of reports on various aspects of dating methods. This work was published in two volumes.[2] Because of the importance of the work, yet its inaccessibility to the layman, Dr. Don DeYoung wrote a simplified version of the study.[3] This latter work is essential reading for anyone who wants to come to grips with what creation science has to say about radiometric dating. Of particular interest to us in this section is a study on zircon crystals carried out by Dr. Russell Humphreys, and published in the RATE books. These crystals are found in micas in granite. They contain measurable amounts of

Zircon crystal

U-238. The zircons in the RATE study had a radiometric U-Pb "age" of 1.5 billion years.

As shown in the sequence above, every U-238 atom that decays forms a Pb-206 atom, but also produces 8 He atoms. The radiometric dating assumes that all the lead in the zircon crystal came from uranium. Therefore, the

1. The RATE Project, http://www.icr.org/research/rate/.
2. Larry Vardiman, Andrew A. Snelling, and Eugene F. Chaffin, editors, *Radioisotopes and the Age of the Earth* (Dallas, TX: Institute for Creation Research, 2000), Volumes 1 & 2.
3. Donald DeYoung, *Thousands . . . not Billions* (Green Forest, AR: Master Books, 2005).

crystal should have produced 8 He atoms for every one Pb atom. Of course, there was less helium than this in practice, because some of the helium had diffused, rather like a children's balloon, having hit the ceiling of the room. The balloon does not stay up forever but eventually returns to the ground, as the helium diffuses through the balloon's elastic skin. The calculated amount of helium (eight times the lead atoms) minus the actual amount of helium would be the diffused helium. If this figure is divided by 1.5 billion years, the diffusion rate (diffusivity) in an evolutionary model is calculated. The same amount of diffused helium divided by 6,000 years gives a creationist diffusivity. Other crystals were also measured, taken from different depths of rock, which therefore had different temperatures. A graph was then plotted of diffusivity against temperature, for both evolutionist and creationist models, and this graph is reproduced here, taken from a report in the *Journal of Creation*.[4] Experiments were also commissioned to determine the actual

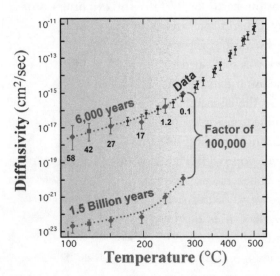

diffusivity of helium from zircon crystals at higher temperatures. There was an enormous difference between the evolutionist and creationist diffusivity, so it was interesting to see whether the experimental results would fit with the evolutionist curve or the creationist curve. As can be seen in the graph, the actual experimental results were an almost perfect fit to the creationist diffusivities, lending strong support to the idea that the crystals were only 6,000 years old, and not 1.5 billion years old.

However, this huge discrepancy leads us to a very important question, which in turn leads us to a startling new conclusion about radioactivity. How did the evolutionary researchers, using U-Pb dating, get their answer so badly wrong? Are they incompetent?

---

4. Russell Humphreys, "Helium Evidence for a Young World Continues to Confound Critics," 2008, http://creation.com/helium-evidence-for-a-young-world-continues-to-confound-critics, accessed 2/14/2012.

The answer is "No!" Of course, they are not incompetent. These are researchers of the highest order, able to perform difficult experiments with high levels of accuracy. They measured the amounts of each atomic species as near perfectly as could be. But in calculating a radiometric age from their measurements, they had to make some assumptions. There must have been an issue with these assumptions.

The three assumptions of radiometric dating are these:

1. The radioactive decay rate (or half-life) must have remained constant.

2. There must have been no lead in the crystals at the start of the process.

3. There must have been no loss or gain of lead.

Assumption 2 is irrelevant in this case, because the lead quantity assumption would be the same in both evolutionary and creationist models. As for assumption 3, with the impermeability of the micas surrounding the zircons, we can safely assume little or no leeching of lead. Therefore, we are faced with the startling conclusion that the half-life of lead has not always been constant. At some point in the natural history of these crystals, the half-life must have shot up to a much greater rate. Second Peter 3 criticizes those who assume uniformitarianism, so Humphreys concludes that the half-life of U-238 must have been far higher at creation than it is today, and again at the outbreak of the Flood. Humphreys has suggested that this accelerated radioactive decay could explain a lot of phenomena in the solar system, as well as on earth: triggering the events that led to the catastrophic plate tectonics, as well as causing nuclear events, causing cratering on the moon and certain planets.[5] This could also have been the cause of the reduction in longevities after the Flood, compared with those before the Flood.

Summary and Conclusion

It is not that the evolutionary time scales in radiometric dating methods do not work. It is that they are based on illogical and unprovable assumptions. Their uniformitarian presuppositions do not explain certain phenomena,

---

5. Russell Humphreys, "Accelerated Nuclear Decay," in Larry Vardiman, Andrew A. Snelling, and Eugene F. Chaffin, editors, *Radioisotopes and the Age of the Earth* (Dallas, TX: Institute for Creation Research, 2000), Vol. 1, p. 357.

such as helium diffusivity in zircons. Therefore, a catastrophic presupposition makes much more sense. In other words, once the Flood is factored into the equation, all our results work sensibly and are consistent with the biblical account of history.

Chapter 14

During the Flood

As earth scientists of the 18th and 19th centuries were beginning to doubt the Bible's time scales, there were some compromisers who tried to explain that there could have been a worldwide Flood as well as millions of years of rock formation. These scientists placed the fossils at millions of years, as did the more radical uniformitarians. Yet scriptural geologists had insisted that the Flood was the cause of the majority of the world's fossils, whereas the uniformitarians believed that the fossils were the result of long-age processes. The compromisers, therefore, had to suggest a Flood that did not cause the fossils to be made. For this reason, they suggested a tranquil Flood. Such a tranquil Flood would have been like gently filling a bathtub. The water would slowly rise and then fall, causing very little to happen below the surface. This extraordinary view nevertheless persists to this day in people's misconceptions about the Flood. It is probably the source of the scoffers' most frequent accusation against Flood geologists about how they expect water to cover Everest. They expect that the water simply rose bit by bit and covered Everest, and then somehow disappeared, presumably down a giant plug-hole at the bottom of the Marianas Trench!

This tranquil Flood model does not fit with reality or our observations of modern floods. It is also not suggested in the Bible. For this reason, it will be interesting to look at what sort of processes might have occurred beneath the water.

Time Scale for the Flood

Genesis 7:12 and 17 suggest that the rain was falling for 40 days. But Genesis 7:24 says that the waters prevailed for 150 days. Therefore, the waters must have continued to rise for 110 days after the rain stopped. This non-raining prevailing seems to be in two parts, as described in 7:18–19.

(18) The waters prevailed and greatly increased on the earth, and the ark moved about on the surface of the waters.

(19) And the waters prevailed exceedingly on the earth, and all the high hills under the whole heaven were covered.

There is no indication as to how much time was required in each of these two sections, so we are going to assume 60 days and 50 days. After these 150 days, there were two more periods of 110 days — the first 110 days, when the ark rested and then a further 110 days as the water receded from the earth.

There must have been many processes, some of them violent, occurring during these periods of time. For example, it is our contention that the Flood water had not actually gone anywhere but was all still there. Therefore, the land had risen and the oceans deepened in order to account for the increased water quantity. These processes must have happened as the waters receded.

Biblical Geology Model

Dr. Tas Walker has produced a model according to these time scales, and has described the very different sorts of rocks that could have been produced in each of these stages. It needs to be emphasized that Dr. Walker's model actually encompasses all rock formations, from the creation week onward, but in this chapter I am going to concentrate only on the material concerning the Flood. Dr. Walker refers to his model as the biblical geology model, because it classifies different types of rock according to these stages and phases in the Flood, rather than by old-earth geological "ages."[1] The descriptions of the rock formations on the following page are all taken from Walker's model, as described on his website.

Walker has suggested that we can define two stages for the Flood. These would be the inundatory stage and the recessive stage. In the inundatory stage, the waters would have been increasing, while in the recessive stage,

---

1. Tas Walker, "Biblical Geology," http://biblicalgeology.net/Model/Development-of-Model. html, accessed 2/14/2012. Scientists continue to debate these and other models.

the waters would have been receding. Walker then divides these stages into phases. He suggests three phases in the inundatory stage — eruptive, ascending, and zenithic. The recessive stage is divided into two phases: the abative phase and the dispersive phase.

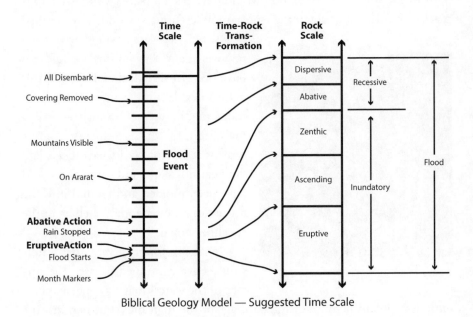

Biblical Geology Model — Suggested Time Scale

Inundatory Stage

The inundatory stage, as its name suggests, is that period of time when the Flood waters were rising. As we have seen, Scripture references suggest splitting this stage into three phases.

The *eruptive phase* was that period that initiated the Flood. In Genesis 7:11–12, we read:

> In the six hundredth year of Noah's life, in the second month, the seventeenth day of the month, on that day all the fountains of the great deep were broken up, and the windows of heaven were opened. And the rain was on the earth forty days and forty nights (Genesis 7:11–12).

Although the period of time is recorded in Scripture, according to the length of time that it rained (Genesis 7:17), the primary rock-building event in this stage would have been the breaking open of the fountains of the deep. During this phase, a great deal of seismic and volcanic activity would have begun. The processes involved are covered in the chapter on catastrophic plate tectonics.

The *ascending phase* is the period when the water would have continued to rise. At this time, presumably, land would still have been visible above parts of the water, and the Flood would have been a planet-wide dangerous maelstrom. The last remaining, more mobile animals would have reached

Syncline

peaks, but the waters would have risen to cover them. Such animals would not have been fossilized, therefore, and this helps to explain the paucity of fossils of more mobile creatures, such as mammals, and, of course, humans. A great deal of sediment could have been laid down at this stage, and some of it could have been molded and faulted into the formations we see today, such as in the syncline shown.

In the *zenithic phase*, the waters would have continued to rise. The surface of the waters may have been apparently less violent because of the coverage of the high hills, but beneath the surface a great deal of further sedimentation would have occurred.

Recessive Stage

As the waters receded, it is possible that activity became apparently less violent. This is known as the *abative phase*. Rocks that had been laid down earlier would have been continually "weathered" and eroded during this period. Some of the newer rocks could have been laid on previously rotated rocks, giving rise to the many so-called unconformities that can be found throughout the world.

Finally, the land would have appeared. As the land was thrust upward, water would have run off the land in the final *dispersive phase* of the Flood. At this point, canyons could have been carved out of the land. Not all canyons were necessarily formed at this phase, however. Some would have been formed in the post-Flood *residual phase*, as trapped areas of water broke free and carved out new canyons. It is possible that the Grand Canyon is the most spectacular example of this recessive dispersal of waters, although there are some creationists who date the Grand Canyon to the immediate post-Flood period.

For completion, it should be mentioned that Walker also refers to the *new world era* being divided into the *residual phase*, mentioned above, and the *modern phase*. The residual phase would have consisted of events such as the Missoula Flood, which covered large areas of North America.[2] The modern phase consists of the present-day, slow geological processes. Modern, secular geologists make the error of assuming that everything they observe in this modern phase is applicable to the entire geological history of the earth.

Siccar Point

An excellent test case to show the power of this biblical geology model is the study of Siccar Point. This geological feature is an icon of old-earth geology. It is the famous place where James Hutton is alleged to have formulated his uniformitarian theory of rock formation.

Siccar Point is situated on the coast of Scotland, about 40 miles east of Edinburgh. In 1788, it was visited by the Scottish lawyer and amateur geologist James Hutton (1726–1797). In his drawing of the Siccar Point rock formation, Hutton has clearly shown the vertical Silurian greywacke layers, covered by nearly horizontal Devonian sandstones.

James Hutton

The current evolutionary age for the greywacke is 425 million years, while the sandstone is supposed to be 345 million years old. During the period between these formations, the lower rock is thought to have been tilted, and then eroded. Evolutionists cannot provide an adequate explanation for why there is a missing 80 million years. Such a missing period of time is known as an unconformity, and unconformities are very common around the world, causing severe problems for old-earth explanations of their origins.

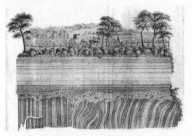

Hutton's unconformity

Tas Walker has also studied this formation and has come up with a more logical explanation. He comments:

Not only were the lower rocks deposited quickly, but they were folded while they were still soft and contained abundant water. The

2. Michael J. Oard, "Only One Lake Missoula Flood," *Journal of Creation* 14(2) (August 2000): 14–17.

beds do not indicate evidence of brittle fracture. So they must have been folded while still plastic. Also, as a result of the folding, the rocks changed (metamorphosed) and new minerals such as mica grew in them. Metamorphic reactions need abundant water if they are to proceed. All this means that there was not much time between deposition and folding.

Another evidence of catastrophe that Hutton missed was the contact between the upper and lower sandstones. He interpreted the contact as a long time-break between the folding and deposition of the next layer of rock. However, where the lower vertically bedded rocks are exposed to the weather in the area, pronounced differential erosion is evident. . . . The softer shale erodes from between the beds of the harder greywacke, which stand out like ribs across the countryside.

However, the contact shows no differential weathering (figure 9), which indicates that the erosion was by catastrophic processes, unlike the gradual erosion of the countryside today. Also, there is no evidence of a soil layer at the contact, as would be expected if the rocks had been eroded by normal weathering.[3]

Walker goes on to explain that the lower rocks were laid down early in the Flood, tilted and eroded rapidly. Then the upper rocks were laid down onto the eroded surface. Using the biblical geology model, it is possible that the greywacke is an inundatory rock — possibly ascending, while the sandstone is possibly an abative rock. Walker concludes his article thus:

Hutton based his conclusion about the age of the earth on wrong assumptions and a wrong interpretation of the rocks. If only he had believed the Bible and looked at the rocks more closely, he would have seen that Siccar Point is excellent evidence of global catastrophe. When we examine the rocks of Siccar Point, it would be hard to find a clearer testimony of Noah's Flood in the geologic record.[4]

Summary and Conclusion

A great deal of rock formation must have occurred while the Flood waters were on the earth. The Flood was not a tranquil event, but an event

3. Tas Walker, "Unmasking a Long Age Icon," *Creation* 27(1) (December 2004): 50–55.
4. Ibid.

of great violence. The evidence for such a worldwide Flood is all around us, including the evidence usually thought by some to support an old-world view. We have seen how a biblical method of classifying rocks can be developed, and how this better explains the formation of such rocks than the old-earth uniformitarian models.

Chapter 15

The Ice Age

Physical education was not my favorite subject in school. It is not that I did not enjoy sports — I was just not very good at them, whereas most of my friends were. Our PE teacher seemed to fit all the stereotypes of PE teachers everywhere. Our math teachers were really smart, our chemistry teacher had published peer-reviewed papers, and our English teacher had a PhD in something to do with the finer points of Shakespeare, or something clever! But what qualifications did a PE teacher need?

Just in case you are a PE teacher, let me emphasize that I now know, having worked alongside PE teachers during my years as a schoolteacher, that PE teachers are highly qualified. But please don't let my adult diminution of prejudice spoil a good story!

Mr. Sugden (not his real name — he might be reading this, and find my address!) was not built like a math graduate or English doctor. He was built more like a tank. His sort of PE was not about speed. He would not have won a 100-meter sprint. It was rumored, however, that he had won a bronze for Britain in judo at the Tokyo Olympics. His pupils were just glad they didn't live in whatever countries the silver and gold medal winners came from. If we answered him back in class — or, more likely, just breathed a bit too much — then he would hold a lock of our hair and instruct us to rotate our head until the pain at the roots was excruciating and we thought our scalp was going to be twisted off in one piece. Come to think about it, I never actually saw him do this, but a friend in another class swore it was true. Looking back on it now, I can't actually remember him doing anything mean, but we never crossed him to find out if the rumors were true. As I said, he was built like a tank.

His conversation was monosyllabic except for the occasional attempt at bigger words, which sounded comical, but we wouldn't have dared laugh or we'd have had to run an extra mile in the cross-country running class.

As was often the case with PE teachers of that era, he also taught geography, which gave him the opportunity to attempt the big words that would have destroyed the classroom discipline of anyone slightly less tough. I remember a field trip in the Yorkshire Dales. We stood at the top of Malham Cove, gazing over the cliff edge into the U-shaped valley below as Mr. Sugden delivered his lecture.

"Right, lads! Shee this? Shee all that there?"

He asked this last rhetorical question, with his inability to enunciate the letter *s*, while sweeping majestically with his enormous hand, each finger thicker than my scrawny teenage arm, trying to take in the U-shaped valley but actually taking in everything else as well from horizon to horizon.

"It'sh all glay-shull. Got it? It'sh all glay-shull. What is it, lads?" After all, he wanted to make sure we got the point.

"It's all glacial, Mr. Sugden, sir!" we chanted in unison, with sufficient enthusiasm, not knowing whether a slight indication of lack of attention would cause him to push one of us to a closer look at the U-shaped valley below.

And so it was! It was most definitely all glacial. Or was it? Did the Ice Age really happen? After all, weren't we taught that the ice ages occurred repeatedly over millions of years, and as a creationist don't I have to reject that opinion?

Evidence of Glaciation

Malham Cove, North Yorkshire, UK

While I may have painted Mr. Sugden as a somewhat intellectually challenged teacher of physical education, the evidence he offered was undeniable. The little stream that emerged from a small cave at the foot of Malham Cove could not possibly have carved the U-shaped valley that we observed. It made more sense to suppose that the

job had been done more cata-
strophically by traveling ice, of
the sort found today in Green-
land and Iceland, or the Alps.

Aletsch Glacier, Alps, Switzerland

One of the features of
present-day glaciers is that they
leave behind piles of debris,
known as moraines. Two well-
known types of moraine are
terminal moraines, which build
up at the end of a glacier, and
lateral remains, which build up
at the sides. The latter can often be
discovered in areas where today there
are no glaciers, such as in Glen Isla in
Scotland. Such features, as well as the
classic U-shaped valleys, suggest that
the landscape was indeed carved out
by icy glaciers.

So how does this affect our creationism? If we concede that there
really was an Ice Age, are we throwing
out the Flood with the Floodwater?

Lateral moraine, upper reaches of Glen
Isla, Scotland
(Image by Gwen and James Anderson)

A Post-Flood Ice Age

Of course, the answer to the above question is — no. One creationist
who has probably done more research than any other on the whole modeling of a possible post-Flood Ice Age is Michael Oard. He has written numerous learned articles modeling the effects that such an Ice Age would have
had, and explaining how it could have occurred.

In a sense, the Ice Age was nothing particularly unusual. There is ice and
glaciation around both poles today. The concept of an Ice Age is that this ice
must have existed at more southerly latitudes in the Northern Hemisphere
than today — and possibly more northerly latitudes in the Southern Hemisphere, though suitable Southern Hemisphere latitudes tend to be more
covered with ocean than in the north.

According to Oard, an Ice Age would require huge amounts of precipitation at aerial temperatures sufficiently low to form snow. He postulates

that such conditions could have been created in the immediate aftermath of a global flood. This is how Oard suggests the Ice Age could have developed:

> Crustal movements would have released hot water from the earth's crust along with volcanism and large underwater lava flows, which would have added heat to the ocean. Earth movement and rapid Flood currents would have then mixed the warm water, so that after the Flood the oceans would be warm from pole to pole. There would be no sea ice. A warm ocean would have had much higher evaporation than the present cool ocean surface. Most of this evaporation would have occurred at mid and high latitudes, close to the developing ice sheets, dropping the moisture on the cold continent. This is a recipe for powerful and continuous snowstorms that can be estimated using basic meteorology. Therefore, to cause an ice age, rare conditions are required — warm oceans for high precipitation, and cool summers for lack of melting the snow. Only then can it accumulate into an ice sheet.[1]

Warmer-than-present oceans evaporating extensively into a cooler-than-present atmosphere provides Oard's recipe for an Ice Age. His more detailed articles go on to show calculations that the current thickness of ice in polar regions could have built up in less than 500 years, rather than the millions of years proposed by secular geologists. Such secular geologists also claim that the Ice Age would have needed to last for hundreds of thousands of years. Oard shows that, if his post-Flood model is used, the ice would have already been on retreat after 200 years, with the Ice Age lasting no longer than 700 years. We are reminded once again that the secular scoffers have willfully ignored the evidence of the Flood, as the Apostle Peter predicted in 2 Peter 3.

The Bible was written in areas that would not have been greatly affected by the Ice Age. Nevertheless, we see some circumstantial evidence for the Ice Age in the Book of Job, which is probably the earliest written book in the Old Testament, and details events that probably occurred concurrently with Genesis 36. In Job 38:19–20, we read:

> From whose womb comes the ice? And the frost of heaven, who gives it birth? The waters harden like stone, and the surface of the deep is frozen (Job 38:29–30).

1. Michael Oard, "Where Does the Ice Age Fit?" in Ken Ham, editor, *The New Answers Book 1* (Green Forest, AR: Master Books, 2007).

We suspect that the area in which the events of Job took place was probably not far from present-day Israel, or the Fertile Crescent, so the existence of such icy features would not be usual today.

Multiple Ice Ages

So far we have referred to THE Ice Age, singular. Yet most old-earth geologists will tell us that the Ice Age to which we refer was simply the most recent of many ice ages in the earth's natural history. Such scientists remind one of the early catastrophists, like Georges Cuvier, who believed that Noah's Flood was merely the most recent of a whole series of global floods to have swept the earth. It seems to be increasingly difficult for scientists to accept the concept of unique occurrences.

In his book *Frozen in Time*, Oard has discussed these theoretical earlier ice ages. He showed that the supposed evidence for earlier ice ages can easily be explained by the one Ice Age — once we understand its unique post-Flood conditions — or by other geological processes. He concludes:

> It seems that geologists have developed too strong a bias toward ancient ice ages to seriously consider other mechanisms for the observed rocks.
>
> The very dynamic Genesis flood produced rapid sedimentation and landslides of unstable sediments. These landslides could duplicate the large scale of some of these "tillites." Landslides would be caused by tectonic motion and huge earthquakes that occurred during the Flood. It is known that the larger the landslides, the farther they travel. Hence, monstrous Flood landslides are bound to cause some unconsolidated sediments to slide long distances and come to rest on nearly level strata, as is observed in these supposed ancient ice age deposits.[2]

Conclusions

The Ice Age can easily be modeled by reference to what we have worked out about the Flood. One of the by-products of this discussion is a reminder that we need not be afraid of scientific evidence. What we need to do is to view that evidence through the correct, biblical paradigm, which in this case must make reference to the catastrophic events of the Global Flood.

---

2. Michael Oard, *Frozen in Time* (Green Forest, AR: Master Books, 2004).

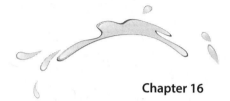

Chapter 16

Short Stories

Fiction can present powerful truths at times. There were a number of issues pertaining to life immediately before the Flood that I wanted to get across to the reader. Yet to simply use more fact-based chapters would not, it seemed to me, have been productive, as I would not have communicated the emotions or the personal issues required.

For these reasons, it seemed right to include some fiction. I spent a few weeks working out how I was going to frame the fiction, until I came across a suggestion that in some legends, Naamah, the daughter of Lamech and Zillah, might have been Ham's wife. Please do not misunderstand my purpose. I am not completely wedded to the idea that Naamah and Ham were married. Other traditions suggest that she was Noah's wife, while still others suggest other ideas. Remember that these stories are fictional!

Nevertheless, with the crossing of generations, it is completely possible that the four children of Lamech mentioned in Genesis 4 (this is not the same Lamech as Noah's father) could have been contemporaneous and similar in age to the sons of Noah. This led to the idea of producing four monologues, expressing the thoughts and activities of each of these children of Lamech. They lived in an unholy world and had an unholy father so they were likely to be deeply unholy themselves. Even if we assume that Naamah was Ham's wife and was therefore saved, it is clear that the other three would have perished. I hope the reader does not find my conclusions to their stories too unsatisfactory, particularly the one case where the outcome is not certain. If I haven't tied everything down quite as you would like, please remember, these are stories. The truths that they contain remain truths, however.

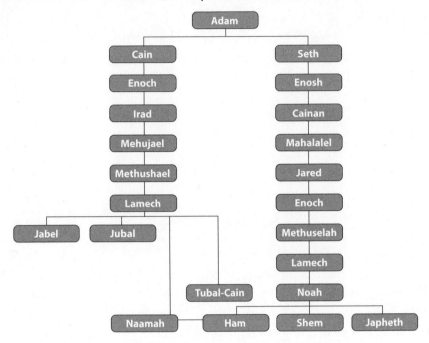

Jubal's Story — Fiction

My father scares me sometimes. Actually, he scares me pretty much all of the time, if I'm honest. I don't like the shouting and I don't like the physical stuff. As long as I can remember, he has pushed me around.

He did the same with all of us. As soon as my brother Jabal was old enough, he was off away from the family home. Anyway, Jabal was a big fellow and more able to take care of himself. I just wanted a quiet life, together with my music.

Father was never really much keen on my music. I remember once making a flute, and he snapped it in half.

"Take that awful racket away from me!" he thundered. So I resolved not to make music in his presence.

I never really understood why I had two mothers. Father had been the first person to take two women — at least officially, though a number of his close relatives had had second women that their wives did not know about. Father decided to make this "above board," even though some of the

Sethite preachers would criticize his lifestyle — so long as they were safely out of his reach! Of course, since Father had taken his second, younger wife, other men who liked to copy Father to stay in his good favor had done likewise.

We lived quite a long distance from Eden, where legend has it that everything began. I don't know whether to believe the legends. It is rumored that the founder of our people, Cain, had even once spoken with the Great Spirit, whom superstitious people say made the world, but there is no evidence of that. Cain died a few years ago, a haunted and miserable figure. There had even been a few attempts to kill him, but they had all failed. No one else seems to have heard of anyone talking to a Great Spirit, so it seems very unlikely to me.

We even live quite a distance from Cain's city, Enoch. That puts us toward the edge of the tropical forest. Very few people have been into the tropical forest, but I am one of them.

After Father broke my flute, I wanted to make a new one. I had heard that a very hard and heavy wood could be found in the tropical forest, so I went off to explore.

I soon found the wood that I had been looking for. It was from a gopher tree. This tall tree grew straight and true and had fern-like fronds for branches. I quickly snapped off one of the fronds and shaped it with the knife that my younger brother, Tubal-Cain, had made. The inside of the woody frond could easily be removed, leaving me with a hollow flute. I dug a single hole through the wood, near to one end, and placed the hole near my lips and blew. It made a pleasingly mellow whistle. I pocketed the new flute. When I got home I would balance this mouth-hole more carefully, and measure out new finger holes.

A noise behind me gave me a start. It was one of the large, bipedal grindles that lived in the tropical forest. With powerful back legs but flimsy forearms, it was a majestic sight. It did not occur to me to be afraid, because I had heard that my grandfather had kept one of these beasts. I was just about to run to greet the creature, when I noticed its mouth was covered in something red. For some reason, I crouched behind the gopher tree as the animal lifted its head and gave a loud roar. Lying by its feet was a huge behemoth, but its neck was bent at an unusual angle. That was the source of the red stuff. It was the blood of life. I had heard people say that in the forest some animals had started to eat other animals, but the reality was terrifying. I ran.

As I emerged from the forest, I could tell that there was an altercation happening. There stood my father, holding a wretched youth — my good friend Joktan — by the ear.

"I'm sorry, Mr. Lamech," Joktan was saying. "I was trying to catch a rabbit. I did not realize that my arrow would be so off-target."

That should settle it, I thought. Had I not also had to apologize to Father, for my mischief?

But Father continued. "Saying a word like sorry is not enough. Sorry is for wimps. I am no wimp, even if you did attempt to wound me." So saying, he clutched at his arm, from which dropped more blood than I had seen in the forest. Then he picked up the unfortunate Joktan's arrow and drove it into my friend's heart, who sank to his knees, then slumped to the ground. I also slumped to the ground in a faint.

When I came to a few minutes later, Father was calling over my mothers, my brothers, and my sister. He snarled at me. "Stay awake, musician boy! You might just learn something."

"Everyone had better be careful around me. I am a strong man. Father Cain always said that the Great Spirit would avenge him seven times if anyone killed him. Well, we all know that the Great Spirit is just a myth. But I have Great Spirit, and what I say will definitely happen. If Cain was to be avenged seven times, then I will avenge myself seventy-seven fold. You know that I can do it. After all, I killed this worm because he wasn't careful enough. No one will draw my blood and live!"

It is well past time that I moved away. I cannot live here, for fear that I will accidentally do something terminally to arouse Father's anger against me. If he could kill my friend, I reckon that he could kill me.

Tubal-Cain's Story — Fiction

My sister is a princess. That must be quite literally true. She isn't the daughter of a king. No, she's the daughter of a tyrant. But at least she has married a prince. He isn't really the son of a king either, in the normal sense of the word, but then we don't have any real princes in the world at the moment — or at least we didn't. But my sister's husband will certainly be a prince in the world and she will be a princess, and their children will have wealth beyond their wildest imaginings. That is, once they have children, which they don't at the moment. They said they were waiting for the new world, and now that new world seems pretty close.

But I'm getting ahead of myself. I think you have heard from my brother. He recorded a journal around the time that our Dear Beloved Father (I hope you note the sarcasm) pretty much turned himself into God and devil all rolled into one. Of course, Father didn't believe in God. Nor did my kindly, but self-absorbed brothers. But I believe in Him — not that it makes any difference now.

Lamech ruled with an iron fist, but that iron was smelted by me. I have always had a fascination for metals. I remember the first time I was given a rock, in which could be seen the gleaming nuggets of the metal that we call gold. I loved that metal. It shone and sparkled. It was I who first hit on the idea of using heat to melt the nuggets out of the rock, and I who skimmed the dross off the liquid metal surface to make it pure.

Heat produced wonderful things, and the rocks contained wonderful things. It seemed logical that the colored minerals in the rocks could also be heated, but I knew that they were no use by themselves — they needed something to react with. Wood charcoal made a perfect accompaniment to the green malachite, the lustrous cassiterite, and the dark gray galena. From these I was able to obtain copper, tin, and lead; beautiful metals in their own right, but so useful when mixed. I discovered that a small measure of tin mixed into the copper made a beautiful metal, almost as attractive as gold, but much harder and more durable. I called it bronze.

It seemed natural to try to make the heat gradually hotter and hotter, and blowing air into the fire produced the extra heat required. It was a complex process that I developed, which eventually extracted the king of manufacturing metals, iron, from hematite. It was worth the effort, because I could cast and sharpen this metal to make implements of great utility, such as plates to eat from and structures for our buildings. The knives that I made could be used to cut ropes and plants — but Father used them to kill people, and soon others followed suit.

Our world became a world of violence, where men of science like myself needed to hide away.

My sister Naamah was always a special girl. She was the youngest of the four of us, and certainly had the greatest charm. When she smiled, her eyes sparkled and her dimples deepened. Young men fell over each other to be at her side. The only good thing that Father ever did was to protect her virtue — though, as with everything else, he achieved this end by shedding the blood of enough young men for them to give up the chase.

This, of course, made any serious suit to my sister almost impossible, but young Ham caught her attention. I remember the first time she introduced me to him. I had to follow her a couple of miles through the dense undergrowth of the tropical forest, watching out for the behemoths and the grindles, until I saw the most remarkable structure I had ever seen.

Of course, the huge wooden vessel was very nearly complete by this time, and Noah and his family and their employees had been hard at work on it for over 100 years. Naamah took my hand and led me to a good-looking dark-faced man, whom she introduced to me, shyly.

"You will have heard of our father, Lamech," I said. It was more of a statement than a question. Everyone had heard of the tyrant of the East, who had led the world into polygamy and violence. "If you value your life, you will be careful how you treat my sister."

"That is exactly how I shall be," said Ham, and at the sound of his voice, I knew immediately that here was a likeable young man, with whom I could trust my sister.

"Ham knows about the Great Spirit," said my sister. "Except, you don't call Him the Great Spirit, do you?"

"No," said Ham. "He is God — or sometimes we call Him Yahweh, when we speak to Him."

"Speak to Him?" I raised an eyebrow. "Do you actually believe those old myths?"

Ham frowned. "They are not myths. God is the one who made this entire world, from nothing, and it is He who has given my father the task of building this ark to save all those who will trust in Him from the coming judgment."

Now I had to laugh out loud! "Nothing made this world, young Ham!" I exclaimed. "Everything that you see is the product of scientific processes. I know! I'm a scientist, and I make new materials from old. New animals have just developed from old over the eons of time."

"A lot of people think that," agreed Ham. "But at least stay and listen to how my father explains it."

Naamah nodded enthusiastically. "Every day, father Noah stops work on the ark and talks to his employees and the crowds that gather. A lot of people come to hear him. He is a very inspiring speaker! Look, he's about to begin now."

Reluctantly, I allowed myself to be persuaded to stay awhile. Quite a crowd had gathered. Eventually, Noah stood, and the crowd began to settle.

"There are a lot of new people here today," he began, "So I will relate God's purposes from the beginning. We are all descended from one man and one woman, who lived in Eden. God created the world to be perfect. In order for the world to remain perfect, Adam and Eve simply had to choose to obey God. God gave them a law — that they were not to eat the fruit of the tree of the knowledge of good and evil. Eve was tempted to eat by the devil, who was in the form of the serpent. Adam, however, was not deceived, but he ate the fruit anyway. He was therefore in debt to God, because he had sinned — that is, he had broken God's law. We have inherited that debt, and also that sinful nature."

"What is he talking about?" I whispered. "Adam and Eve weren't really made by God. They just developed from other animals."

"Hush!" responded Naamah.

Noah was continuing. "God has foretold that He will punish sin by flooding this entire world. All the high hills will be covered, and no one remaining on the earth will survive. He promised that the Great Flood would come to end the world the same year that my grandfather Methuselah died — and he died just three months ago. So the Flood is coming."

The crowd was beginning to murmur. I heard some sarcastic laughter.

"But you don't need to die! I have been building this ark, according to God's instructions. There are three decks in there. There will be one whole deck just for people. We can fit a lot of people on there. All you need to do is to have the humility to admit that you are a sinner, and trust in God, and He will allow you on to this ark."

"Rubbish!" shouted someone. "There's no water here! You are hundreds of miles from water! How are you going to drag that big boat through the tropical forest past the grindles?"

Noah gave an impassioned cry. "Why would you want to choose death instead of life? Why would you want to die? God always does what He says He will do. The water is coming, and there is no other way of escape for you."

"I've heard enough," I hissed to Naamah. "I'm going home, and I'd advise you to get home pretty fast, if you don't want the Tyrant on your back."

One day, Naamah did not come back. Father was angry, but there was nothing that he could do. Naamah had legally married Ham. She told me she had repented of her sin, and was going to get on board the ark with Ham and his family. So she will be a princess. She and her prince, together with his two brothers and their wives, will be princes and princesses of the new world, as they populate that place, following God's judgment on this world — a judgment that we simply would not believe in. How could we fail to believe?

"Please think about your sins!" she begged me. "We only have seven more days before the waters come."

"I'm not falling for that nonsense," I replied haughtily. "I'm going back to my metalwork. The future is in metal, not in silly wooden ships going nowhere."

But it wasn't nonsense, was it? There are few places of high ground left, and there are earthquakes and volcanic activity, noise and disaster everywhere. People are dying and animals are dying. I had every opportunity in the world to be saved, but I just would not believe. Is it too late even now? I know that I cannot get to the ark, so I know that I am going to die. I know that I deserve to die for my sins, and I am sorry for them. If I had the chance, I would turn completely from them. Even in this last minute, would He accept my cry and take my soul to be with Him?

Jabal's Story — Fiction

The world is a mess, and it has been a mess for a very long time. If it were not a mess, then the Tyrant would not have so much power.

Excuse me for not having introduced myself properly. My name is not that important, as I have lived alone for many years and will soon die alone.

The Tyrant was my father. I say "was." I do not know if he is still alive, though I pray he has died horribly. The Tyrant thought he was God. He thought he was the world's supreme being. He thought that nothing mattered, except his own power and authority.

My childhood, such as it was, was deeply unhappy. The Tyrant bullied me into doing his will. I know other children who were spanked, but I knew of no one who was beaten, as I was regularly, leaving bruises. My younger brother, Jubal, was also beaten, but he seemed to be able to escape somehow into his music. My mother, Adah, was also beaten regularly if she did not submit quickly and meekly to any degrading thing the Tyrant might have in mind. I had nowhere to escape, especially as I had a shameful secret.

My secret was not as shameful as the Tyrant's, though. I still remember the sting of tears as I learned that I had a younger brother and sister. The Tyrant had been seeing a lady called Zillah in the next town. In itself, this was not unusual — there were other men who cast their favors about, so to speak. It was the Tyrant's lack of shame that was so galling. That fateful day, he brought Zillah and her children with him from the other town and presented them before my poor mother.

"I now have two wives, because your service to me is not enough," he snarled. "You will both live under my roof, and obey me without question. I rule here and I will do whatever I want, when I want."

Strange to say, but Adah and Zillah did not hate each other. Indeed, my mother pitied the younger woman, as she saw in her a version of herself, and the Tyrant was not noticeably kinder or gentler to Zillah than he was to my mother.

One day, when the Tyrant had used a stick on both mothers, I kept out of the way by visiting my clearing in the forest. Here I had installed fencing so that I could keep animals, after the fashion of the Sethites. I had a stone altar, like the Sethites, on which I could light a fire. However, here the similarity ended. I did not use the altar to worship the Great Spirit. I didn't even believe such a Spirit existed. I killed an occasional animal, using a knife that had been fashioned by my industrious half-brother. Then I used the fire to cook portions of it — and I ate pieces of the cooked flesh, like someone might eat rice cakes or rutabagas. It was delicious.

My livestock holding was once visited unexpectedly by a Sethite. Sethites are such tiresome people: opinionated, sanctimonious, and legalistic. Everyone has to follow their rules, or there is no hope for them, apparently. I have come across one group of Sethites who don't appear to be like this. They used to be led by a legendary figure called the Seventh Teacher, but he just disappeared one day, never to be seen again. This Sethite who found me was not of the Seventh Teacher's order. He had come to criticize me.

"Yahweh has forbidden us to eat animals' flesh," he pontificated. "That is a rule for all time."

"Have you tasted it?" I asked.

"Of course not," he responded, offended. "It would be evil to do so."

"How can you know something is evil without trying it?" I teased. I held out a fork with a particularly juicy morsel on it. "Try some!" He came closer, clearly tempted by the savor. At the last minute, however, he threw up his hands and ran off.

Although I had teased him, I was now in a quandary, because he had seen my secret. I tiptoed home.

"Where have you been?" demanded the Tyrant.

"I have been walking in the forest, sir," I stammered.

"You have been seen by a Sethite," he announced. I felt sick inside. What would the Tyrant do to me? Then he surprised me by speaking tenderly. "Don't worry, son. Your secret is safe. I have persuaded him to say nothing."

Puzzled, but relieved, I retired to my chamber. I drew back the covers, and vomited over my sleeping area. There, under the cover, was the bloodied, severed head of the Sethite.

Somehow, I managed to get outside, my head swimming. I knew in my heart that I could not return. Hiding behind doors, I was able to steal a few supplies, and then I headed off, past my livestock pen and thence farther into the forest.

After a couple of days I reached the ocean. The sea looked inviting. But at that point I saw something unusual out to sea. I had always been led to believe that there was only one land mass, but out in the ocean, on the distant horizon, I was sure that I could make out trees.

In retrospect, it was probably a rash decision, but I decided to swim. For the first hour, the other land did not seem to get any nearer. Then, bit by bit, the trees started to take shape, and I realized I was at last getting closer. What I eventually saw astounded me. This was not land! It was a raft of vegetation, with amazing tall but flexible trees.

I hauled myself onto the raft and began to walk in a direction that I can only call inland. Pretty soon I was out of sight of the sea. Small frogs hopped around by my feet and pretty soon I was lost. I sat down under a particularly cool tree and contemplated what I could remember of what the Seventh Teacher had reportedly said. He had spent a lot of time traveling and preaching that God was sending judgment because of our sins, and that this judgment would come the year his son died.

I can't now recall how many years I have been on this floating island. It seems like forever. I found my way back to the edge but could not see the shore of the continent. I have walked for years around the perimeter of this enormous raft but have never seen the land from which I came. So I have had plenty of time to contemplate this Great Spirit whom the Sethites call Yahweh. Something inside me suggests that old man Seth knew something, and so did the Seventh Teacher. But it is better not to dwell on such things. I know I have not always done what I should, and I have broken some of this God's laws, if He exists. But surely, if He exists, He will weigh up the good and bad that I have done, and realize that the rubbish that happened to me was not my fault. Even so, my conscience pricks me, but I tell it to be quiet.

Naamah's Story — Fiction

I am glad I met my husband, Ham. I am also glad I met my father-in-law, Noah. But I am most especially glad that I met my Savior and Redeemer, Yahweh.

My story begins in a complicated family situation — a family that was created in opposition to God's plans for family. Yet when I started to complain to Noah that God had put me in a wicked family, so there was no hope for me, he said that God always had a plan for us, and that I was to come to Him as I was, confessing my sins and asking His forgiveness.

It took so long for this message to sink in.

I remember the day that I first met Noah and his sons. It was Japheth whom I met first. He was a very young man and his eyes sparkled when he laughed. He had pale skin and blue eyes, and he was a complete tease. I had been on one of my solitary walks, because I so needed to be away from my father, as I knew that he would hurt any young man who so much as smiled at me.

Despite his youth, Japheth was already married, and so was his brother, Shem. I liked these women immediately, and realized that they had qualities that I did not have. Shem's wife, Em, I found particularly helpful. She, like me, had an angry past. She had been abandoned by her father. Her mother had found another man, who had, at first, seemed kind to Em and her brother. However, one day when her brother and mother were not around, her stepfather came to her and forced her to lie with him.

I did not know what to say. It turned out that he began to do this repeatedly, and he kept her silence with threats.

One day, she was helping in the fields, and her stepfather tripped over a scythe and badly cut his leg. He cried out for help, but only Em was around.

"Did you kill him?" I asked.

Em paused. "I have to be honest that I thought about it. I badly wanted to kill him, and I could have done it. There was a large rock in the field. In my head, I could see myself lift the rock and smash it down on his skull. Then, I opened my eyes, and I actually saw the rock in my hand and the fear in his eyes. I dropped the rock and ran to the village to get help."

"You ran to the village to get help for the man who took away your childhood?" I was incredulous.

"Don't get me wrong," said Em. "He deserved punishment. But it was not for me to give that punishment. My place was to forgive him."

I could not take this in. "The man was a monster. He deserved to die."

"But not at my hands, Naamah. Do you think I am without guilt myself?"

"You were a child!"

"No, I am not referring to the abuse, which was dreadful. I am talking about my other sins."

"You don't seem like a sinful person to me," I protested.

"No — and one of my problems has been my pride in the way I am. I have not deliberately set out to hurt anyone. I could feel very proud of myself. But that would be like worshiping myself, instead of God. My conscience tells me that we should worship God above everything else."

"Is your conscience really that hard on you?" I asked skeptically.

Em smiled. "What does your conscience tell you, Naamah? Mine tells me that I should not tell lies, but I have. My conscience tells me that I should not steal, but I have taken things that don't belong to me, like from my brother, when he wasn't looking. My conscience tells me that the beauty of sexual relations should only be within marriage."

"But you were abused," I protested again.

"Dear Naamah, let me finish. When Shem and I were getting close, I wanted to lie with him. We did not do so — but I dreamt about it. I did the deed in my head. God sees our inner thoughts."

"If you say that those things are sins, then I have done worse. What hope is there for any of us?"

"By ourselves, there is no hope. We deserve everlasting punishment from God. And God will punish — He has told Father Noah directly that He will send floodwaters to cover this whole earth, and that will be a picture or a reminder of the final destruction that He will one day bring. But God also loves us. After the first man and woman sinned, God immediately promised that He would send a Savior one day. That Savior will be born miraculously, without a human father. Noah has said that this Savior will actually be God Himself in human form."

"How can that happen? How can God become human?"

"I don't know, Naamah, and it is all in the future. But I believe it will happen. The Savior will take the punishment for all our sins, past, present, and future, if we put our trust in God now. He Himself is our Redeemer."

I was stunned at the perfect righteousness of a holy God and at His amazing, unfathomable love for us.

"How do I get my sins forgiven?" I asked.

"You need to repent and trust. Repent and trust. Repent means to be sorry for your sins. But it means more than that. It means actually turning away from those sins in your mind — repudiating them, and being determined to go God's way instead of our own. Then you need to trust that what God says about forgiving your sins is true."

Again, I was silent. "I know it's true, Em. I believe it with all my heart. God must love us so much if He is prepared to do all that for us, despite His righteous anger at sin."

"Indeed, He does, Naamah."

"But what happened to your mother's husband?" I asked.

Em shrugged. "I do not know. He recovered quickly and made his escape. The village elders wanted to kill him, but he was gone. Someone must have helped him."

"Do you honestly feel no bitterness?"

Em paused. "I have forgiven him," she said at last. "But like everyone, I still have a sinful nature. My forgiveness has to be active, because there are some days when I wish all over again that I could have planted the rock in his skull. But then I would have been guilty of murder, as well as lying, stealing, and idolatry. Yet my conscience tells me that all of these sins take us short of God's standards, so I am not really any the less guilty than him. I pray that he might find forgiveness. But if he doesn't, I can only be responsible for my own sins — not his as well."

I thought about my own father. I thought about the beatings, the anger, and the hatred. I thought about the young men that he had wounded or even killed, because of me. And I thought about how I had sometimes felt glad in my heart for what he had done, and I was ashamed.

"I need that forgiveness, Em," I said at last. "I need that forgiveness more than anything else in the world."

"You do indeed."

The rest of the story, you know. I was saved that day, and found forgiveness. Noah told me about the space on the ark for believers. I was going to have a place in my own right! However, as it happened, Ham and I grew close, and married. So I will get to be with my new husband on a difficult, dangerous, but protected voyage, and then I will get to help rebuild a devastated planet.

Regrets? I wish I could have persuaded my brother Tubal, whom I love so much, to see his sins and to repent. Even now, as the waters rise and his death is inevitable, maybe he might find higher ground and trust in God before the waters overtake him. I am convinced that if he does so, God will take his soul to be with Him, even though he is not here on the ark with me. God is merciful to sinners. We do not deserve His love that He has lavished upon us. Praise His holy name!

Chapter 17

The Gospel According to Noah

God sent the Flood for a purpose. In this book we have discussed that the event known as the Flood was a historical event, and that studies of it have scientific credibility. We have also expounded the relevant chapters of Genesis to show that God had a purpose through the Flood.

The New Testament has a great deal to say about the Flood and its relevance to the gospel. It is my contention that part of what God was doing in the Flood was revealing His methods of salvation. The Flood account is a living presentation of the gospel, as it illustrates both the wrath and mercy of God.

For those reasons, this chapter does not contain new information, but rather pulls together previous material, in order to make this presentation of the gospel clear.

All Have Sinned

Since Adam ate the fruit, mankind's nature has been one of rebellion and sin against God. This is the reality of our nature. This does not imply that we behave as badly as it is possible to behave. Many skeptics have complained to me that they are just as good as me. That is probably true. Indeed, it is possible that some of them have behaved better than me. But that is not the point. God does not weigh our good and our bad in the balance.

If He did, it would go badly for us, I can tell you! The Bible states the case honestly.

> All we like sheep have gone astray; we have turned, every one, to his own way; and the Lord has laid on Him the iniquity of us all (Isaiah 53:6).

> For all have sinned and fall short of the glory of God (Romans 3:23).

God's standard for our lives is the Ten Commandments. Try rating yourself against these Commandments, which are found in Exodus 22.

The ninth Commandment says you must not lie. Have you ever told a lie? If so, you are a liar.

The eighth Commandment says you must not steal. Have you ever stolen anything? Be honest! We have already established that you are a liar! If you have stolen something, then you are a thief.

The seventh Commandment says you must not commit adultery. Have you done so? No? Jesus said that whoever looks on someone with lust has already committed adultery in their hearts. If you have done this, then you are an adulterer at heart.

The third Commandment says you must not take the Lord's name in vain. You must not use words like Lord, God, Jesus, or Christ in place of filthy curse words. Have you done this? If so, it is called blasphemy and God takes it very seriously.

These are just four Commandments. There are six more. But James, in his epistle, says that if you are guilty of breaking just one of these, then you are guilty of all of them. Are you a lying, thieving, blasphemous adulterer at heart? You have to face God on Judgment Day with that on your record. If God judges us by those Commandments, will you be innocent or guilty? The Bible says that all liars will have their part in the Lake of Fire; that no thief or adulterer will inherit the Kingdom of heaven; and that God will not hold blasphemers guiltless. You will be guilty. Do you deserve heaven or hell? You deserve hell. And so do I.

That is the state that people were in before the Flood, also.

> Then the Lord saw that the wickedness of man was great in the earth, and that every intent of the thoughts of his heart was only evil continually (Genesis 6:5).

This wickedness of our hearts causes our loving Father God grief.

> And the LORD was sorry that He had made man on the earth, and He was grieved in His heart (Genesis 6:6).

Because God is just, He must punish sin, otherwise He would not be a good Judge. But God also is a God of mercy and love. How can these two aspects of God's nature come together?

In Genesis, God sent the Flood to destroy the world, but he made sure that there was the ark of salvation.

> The ark was being prepared, in which a few, that is, eight souls, were saved through water (1 Peter 3:20).

Those who got on the ark would be saved from the ravages of the Flood. The ark was waterproofed by pitch, but the Hebrew word for pitch is the same as "atonement." Atonement refers to the covering for sins achieved in the Old Testament by the blood of sacrifices. In the New Testament, this atoning sacrifice is made perfect through the shedding of the blood of Jesus, and this has been done once for all on the Cross. The Bible says that without the shedding of blood there is no forgiveness of sins. But the Bible also says that now that Jesus has shed His blood, there is no further need for any other blood sacrifice.

Why did God choose Noah to be saved? Was Noah a really good man? No! After the Flood, we read about mistakes that Noah made. He was a sinner just like you and me. So why was he saved?

> But Noah found grace in the eyes of the LORD (Genesis 6:8).

Ephesians 2:8–9 says:

> For by grace you have been saved through faith, and that not of yourselves; it is the gift of God, not of works, lest anyone should boast.

Noah was saved by grace. Did this grace come by faith, as it is supposed to do in the New Testament? Yes, it did!

> By faith Noah, being divinely warned of things not yet seen, moved with godly fear, prepared an ark for the saving of his household, by which he condemned the world and became heir of the righteousness which is according to faith (Hebrews 11:7).

Noah's righteousness came by faith.

So Noah was a sinner like everyone else before the Flood. The difference was that he had faith, and this came to him by the grace of God. For that reason, he was saved from the judgment of God by the atoning pitch that covered the ark.

Are you a sinner? We have established that you are. Do you deserve hell? We have established that you do. Can you experience the grace of God? Yes — you need to put your faith completely in Jesus, knowing that He can save you as thoroughly as the ark saved Noah.

The ark had a door on it. When it was time for the Flood, Noah did not shut the door himself. God shut him in.

Jesus said:

> I am the door. If anyone enters by Me, he will be saved, and will go in and out and find pasture (John 10:9).

This is why there is no salvation other than through Jesus. It is also why there is complete salvation for those who truly come to Jesus to be saved. You and I and all people are really in the same state as the people before the Flood. I am as much a sinner as anyone else, but I have repented and put my trust completely in Jesus. You need to do the same. You need to repent of your sins — that is, to turn from them completely. And you need to trust in the Savior, Jesus Christ. If you will do that, God will forgive your sins, and you will be shown grace, meaning that you will go, when you die, to the place that you deserve.

God shows mercy and grace. The difference between mercy and grace has been described thus: mercy is not being treated as you deserve; grace is being treated as you do not deserve.

Father, I pray that many who read these words will recognize that they are sinners, and will repent and trust in Your Son for their salvation.

If you are expecting a sinner's prayer to close this chapter, you will look in vain. I do not have a form of words for you to pray. If you had committed adultery, would you really go to your wife and read out an apology from a card? Of course not! If you are genuinely sorry, then you speak from the heart. Some people tell me they don't have the words to pray to God. Then you are not saved and you have not really repented. If you had truly repented of your sins, then the words of repentance would not be hard to find. Go to God by yourself, in person, in private. And don't leave it a moment longer!

Pick up a fossil and look at it. It did not die millions of years ago. It was trapped in the sediment of the Flood, which came because of God's judgment. God will punish sin. But the fact that you can look at the fossil today proves that your ancestors were saved through the Flood. God also sends salvation. The fossil is your reminder of the Good News — the gospel that God saves sinners from hell and takes them to be with Him in heaven. Praise His name!

Appendix

Questions for Study

Small group discussions are always helpful on any aspect of Bible teaching. Learning about the Flood is no exception. For that reason, a few questions are included here on each of the chapters. These questions are not a full study guide, but are designed to stimulate thought. If they are being used in a small group situation, then I would recommend that the leader expand on these questions with some leading questioning.

The DVD series to accompany this book contains a full small-group curriculum covering the issues addressed within the film series (www.creationtoday.org).

Chapter 1 — The World before the Flood

1. Compare and contrast the legacies of Cain and Seth. Was the worship of the Lord genuine among all the descendants of Seth?

2. List the ways in which Lamech's attitude and behavior were wrong. To what extent do we see such errors today?

3. What is your opinion about who the "sons of God" and "daughters of men" were?

4. In what ways was the Flood prophesied?

5. Why did God not destroy the world immediately? Why wait 120 years? What does this teach about the judgment and the mercy of God?

6. What is your opinion about what or who the giants were?

7. Compare and contrast present-day society with the pre-Flood society.

8. What does the account of the Flood teach us about salvation?

Chapter 2 — Preparing for the Flood

1. Noah took over a hundred years to build the ark. What does this tell us about his faithfulness and obedience?

2. Why was Noah saved from the Flood?

3. What does the New Testament tell us about Noah?

4. What does this passage tell us about *how* God saves people?

Chapter 3 — God Remembered Noah

1. Could God have forgotten Noah?

2. What information about the mechanism of the Flood can be gleaned from Psalm 104?

3. What does it mean to say that the ark is a *type* of Christ?

4. God promises to maintain the seasons in Genesis 8:22. What are the implications of that verse to modern concerns in society and science?

Chapter 4 — A Covenant and a Rainbow

1. What does the rainbow symbolize?

2. What commission did God give to Noah?

3. How did human diet change after the Flood? Why?

4. What does this passage teach us about good government?

5. How is God's faithfulness illustrated by the fact that the Flood was global?

6. What mistakes were made by Noah and any of his sons at the end of Genesis 9? What actions were to be commended?

Chapter 5 — The History of the Ancient World

1. When did the early civilizations begin, approximately? What is the biblical reason for your answer?

2. What does Genesis 4 teach us about early cultural developments?

3. Give an overview, in your opinion, on the life and times of Nimrod.

4. What are some of the reasons for re-dating Egyptian history? In what ways does the re-dating help?

5. What does the existence of flood legends in other cultures tell us? What happened to people groups after Babel?

Chapter 6 — Why We Stopped Believing in the Flood

1. Who were some of Steno's contemporaries? In what ways could he be described as the "father of geology"?

2. Why do Hutton's old-earth views undermine belief in the authority of the Bible?

3. Define uniformitarianism. In what ways is this philosophy seen in scientific ideas today?

4. What was Lyell's motivation for old-earth ideas?

5. Describe the work of some of the scriptural geologists.

Chapter 7 — The Flood and the Modern Creationist Movement

1. In your opinion, how important was the book *The Genesis Flood*?

2. Discuss progressive creationism. What are the problems with this approach? What are the problems with the Intelligent Design movement?

3. Why do old-earth views tend to go hand-in-hand with a local Flood philosophy?

4. In what ways did Mount St. Helens help us understand the Flood?

Chapter 8 — How Did the Flood Start?

1. How far should one look for naturalistic explanations for a supernatural event?

2. What should be our starting point as we study the possible mechanism of the Flood?

3. It is suggested that Catastrophic Plate Tectonics owes a great deal to early geologist Antonio Snider-Pellegrini. Why?

4. Why is traditional plate tectonic theory insufficient to explain rock formations? What advantages does CPT have over the traditional model?

5. How could runaway subduction have been the engine to begin Flood processes? What evidence is there for runaway subduction?

6. Why is magnetic striping around the mid-Atlantic ridge better explained by Flood geology than secular geology?

Chaptrer 9 — The Waters Above

1. What is the difference between a scientific model and scriptural truth?

2. What were the scriptural reasons for adopting the canopy theory? What are the scriptural reasons for now rejecting it?

3. How does more recent scientific research eliminate the need for proposing a vapor canopy?

4. Where does Russell Humphreys suggest that the waters above now are?

Chaptere 10 — Fossils

1. Do fossils support evolutionary ideas? Why do evolutionists believe that they do?

2. Does the fossil record show change over time? What are the presuppositions behind this question, and how are they used to challenge the evolutionary view of fossils?

3. How do polystrate fossils cause problems for long-age geologists?

4. Given that the geologic column is not a record of time scale, how do creationists use the column to explain pre-Flood environments? For example, why are dinosaur fossils usually found with gymnosperm plants?

5. What unusual pre-Flood ecosystem was proposed by Dr. Kurt Wise to explain coal formation? What are the reasons for his proposals?

6. Explain how fossils can be used in a gospel presentation.

Chapter 11 — The Design of the Ark

1. What facts do we actually know about the design of the ark? Is it legitimate to research other factors to do with the ark's design?

2. What are the meanings of the terms *rooms*, *window*, and *pitch*?

3. What information can we glean from the relative dimensions of the ark being 300 by 50 by 30 cubits?

4. What are the theological implications of the ark?

Chapter 12 — The Animals Came in Two by Two

1. What misconceptions cause skeptics to ridicule the account of the ark? How do Christians contribute to this ridicule of God's Word?

2. What is the difference between a *kind* and a *species*? How does this affect our ideas about how many animals there would have been on the ark?

3. If the Flood had been a local Flood, would the ark have needed to hold birds?

4. How did kangaroos get from Ararat to Australia? What are the implications of the post-Flood recolonization of the world by animals?

5. How is the concept of a post-Flood Ice Age a useful model for recolonization?

Chapter 13 — Radiometric Dating and the Flood

1. Is carbon dating accurate?

2. In what way is radiometric dating based on the concept of *uniformitarianism*? What does 2 Peter have to say on the subject of uniformitarianism?

3. What are the assumptions behind carbon dating? Even if we believed in an old-earth scenario, why would it not be possible for carbon dating to date anything much older than 60,000 years?

4. Why is helium formed during the radioactive decay of uranium? Why do zircon crystals not retain helium? Do helium diffusion measurements fit better with an evolutionary or a creationist age for the earth?

5. What was the conclusion of the RATE group about the anomalous measurements of U-Pb dating and helium diffusion?

Chapter 14 — During the Flood

1. Explain the biblical reason for Dr. Walker's new classification of sedimentary rocks? Why did he adopt two stages and five phases? What biblical accounts are represented by each of these stages and phases?

2. Describe the rock formations at Siccar Point in Scotland. What did James Hutton conclude about these formations? How does Dr. Walker explain the same formations from a biblical perspective?

Chapter 15 — The Ice Age

1. How do geologists suppose that U-shaped valleys got their shape? What physical evidence is there for glaciation in the past in areas of northern Europe and North America?

2. How could the conditions of the Flood have triggered an Ice Age? Is there any biblical evidence that such an Ice Age happened?

Chapter 17 — The Gospel According to Noah

1. What was God's purpose in sending the Flood? What does the Flood account tell us about human nature?

2. How do we know that we are sinners? What is the biblical definition of sin?

3. Why was Noah saved? Was he a really good person?

4. The ark had a door. Jesus said, "I am the door." What is the connection between these two concepts?

5. How can a sinner be forgiven?

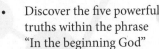

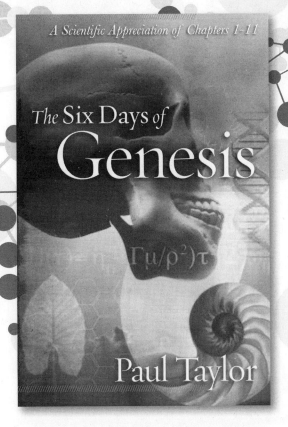

A Scientific Appreciation of Chapters 1-11

The Six Days of
Genesis

$\Gamma \mu / \rho^2) \tau$

Paul Taylor

- Discover the five powerful truths within the phrase "In the beginning God"

- Learn just how closely evolutionists and creationists agree on the division of land and water on the earth.

- Uncover the biblical clue to where energy came from to explore life processes on an earth without form and void.

- Explore whether there is any truth to the re-colonization theory.

Can we really trust Genesis as the literal history of the world? Many modern scholars and scientists would have you believe that you can't, but this fascinating expository study by Paul F. Taylor lays all doubts about the authenticity of the Bible to rest. Follow this spellbinding, verse-by-verse study Taylor takes you on from the Garden of Eden to the Fall to the Table of Nations.

Many Christians are alarmed by the disappearance of true biblical teachings in churches and even in many seminaries across America and Britain, but this much-needed resource for teaching prospective clergy and professors will help to battle the disturbing departure from biblical truth. This exciting new tool is a wonderful aid for those who wish to defend against the evolutionary attacks leveled at them by society and sometimes even by the church.

Master Books®
A Division of New Leaf Publishing Group
www.masterbooks.net

The Six Days of Genesis
Paul F. Taylor
9780890514993 | $13.99

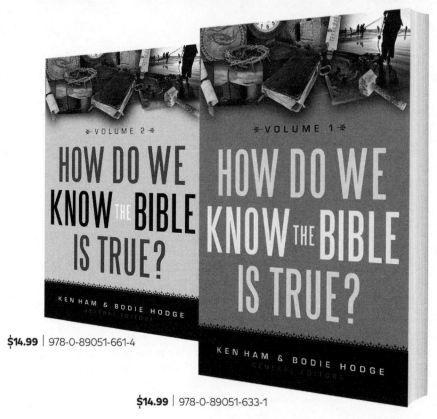